Paul Sheldon

MILESTONES behind the MARQUES

David & Charles

Newton Abbot   London   North Pomfret (VT)   Vancouver

ISBN 0 7153 7267 X
Library of Congress Catalog Card Number : 76-2011

Set in 9D on 10 point Univers
and printed in Great Britain
by Redwood Burn Limited
for David & Charles (Publishers) Limited
Brunel House Newton Abbot Devon

Published in the United States of America
by David & Charles Inc
North Pomfret Vermont 05053 USA

Published in Canada
by Douglas David & Charles Limited
1875 Welch Street North Vancouver BC

Contents

Foreword

by DENIS JENKINSON

To compile a book of data and statistics such as this is a formidable task, especially when it is done without the first-hand knowledge of someone who is part of a team or has access to a manufacturer's records. It is the result of sheer enthusiasm for racing cars, and all credit must be given to the author and his fellow enthusiasts of the Formula One Register for being courageous enough to tackle such a project and to offer some of their findings in book form.

Naturally I am not going to claim to have verified all the facts and figures contained here, although I have read the printer's proofs, as the task of cross-checking everything would not only be an onerous one, but would take as long as Paul Sheldon has spent on the compilation; indeed, I would have been in a position to have written it myself!

The significant fact is that there is someone who is enthusiastic enough about racing cars as animate things to have kept such records and to have produced a book such as this. It was the enthusiasm which Paul Sheldon has for individual cars as living beings that prompted me to write my first book about racing cars nearly thirty years ago, and that same enthusiasm still exists. Even today, when so many people look upon a racing car as a mere 'tool of the trade' for a racing driver, they are so much more than that to me. They have as much personality and individuality as the driver himself and my only regret is that they cannot write their own biographies, for they would have some splendid tales to tell which even those of us who follow their fortunes closely cannot hope to know or reveal.

A racing car is very much like the famous axe that beheaded Mary, Queen of Scots, which since that day has had six new handles and four new heads, yet remains the original axe. During its active life, the racing car may use as many as ten different engines, six different gearboxes, four new 'monocoque' tubs and have the suspension components changed many times, while wheels and tyres are changed continually. Yet the car itself is unchanged, though we would be hard pressed to state categorically which part is the actual 'car'.

To some readers the selection of cars chosen for this book may seem unusual, as most of them were relative failures, but the success and glamour of makes such as Lotus or Tyrrell are all too easy to deal with. It is unlikely that any reader will agree wholeheartedly with the author's choice, but that makes the book all the more interesting. If we all liked the same racing cars or racing teams, life would be very dull and we would just sit around nodding agreement with one another. As it is, each make has its following and when a group of racing car enthusiasts gets together there is seldom a dull moment, as each is ready to defend or extoll his particular choice. Among my own personal favourites dealt with here is the ill fated V8 air-cooled Honda, while others for which I have a preference are the Gurney Eagle-Weslakes and the March 721X, in spite of being very conscious of the shortcomings of both.

The compilation and recording of dates and statistics of racing cars, which provides the nucleus for a book such as this, have to be done from raw enthusiasm, and for this reason alone, if for no other, I am happy to have the opportunity to provide the foreword for this book.

Denis Jenkinson
Crondall
Hampshire

Author's Preface

I must freely admit that the concept of this book was provided by a book entitled *Case History* published many years ago. The idea of following the trail of Grand Prix cars from cradle to grave has appealed to me ever since. Obviously it appeals to others also, as I found in 1962 when I met John Thompson and Duncan Rabagliati who were to become the other two members of the Formula One Register. These two fellow enthusiasts were to be of constant help in the years to come and their assistance in the compiling of this book has been indispensable. Needless to say, any errors there may be are all my own fault and the Register would be pleased to have these mistakes corrected as, of course, the most important factor for us is that the record should be complete and correct. The Register continues to compile statistics of Formula 1 events but also follows Formula 2 and Formula 5000 events with interest. We are at present trying to build up records retrospectively to 1948; any help with this in the way of statistics, old race programmes and memorabilia would be most welcome and, of course, returned intact.

The purpose of this volume is to record in print the detailed history of some of the more interesting models that have appeared and raced to the regulations of Formula 1 from 1966 to 1975. Not all the models have been successful, one or two have been disastrous failures, but all have been genuine attempts and the teams behind them have always fondly believed that next year will be their year. They still try, and thank goodness for that, for Grand Prix racing would be pretty dull with but one team racing if all the others gave up. It seems only fitting that the teams' efforts should be set down as a permanent record of the ingenuity, doggedness and bravery of the motor racing scene which has given me, at least, the greatest pleasure over the last fifteen years.

Paul Sheldon
4, Station Road
Esholt, Shipley
West Yorkshire
England

BRM

Type 153

Type	153
Year of construction	1970
Number made	7
Frame designer	Tony Southgate
Frame	Half length monocoque with sub-frame for front suspension, engine forms rear part of chassis
Front suspension	Double wishbones with outboard coil spring/damper units
Rear suspension	Lower wishbone, upper transverse link, two forward running radius arms with outboard coil spring/damper units
Engine make	BRM
Engine designer	Geoff Johnson
Engine type	142
Engine capacity	2999cc
Cylinders	12 in 60° Vee formation
Bore and stroke	74.1mm x 57.2mm
Valves	2 inlet per cylinder in Vee, 2 exhaust per cylinder laterally
Carburation	Lucas port fuel injection
Ignition	Coil and distributor
Sparking plugs	1 centrally placed plug per cylinder
Camshafts per bank	2 overhead
Gearbox	BRM 131
Brakes	Outboard discs

BRM 153/01 Oliver testing the prototype before its first race appearance in early 1970

The organisation at BRM had for many years seemed cumbersome. This was reflected mainly in the slowness of their decision making and in a tendency to over-reach themselves while, on the other hand, appearing resistant to change. From the beginning they consistently brought out new models too late to be successful. Sometimes such tardiness was overcome, at other times it proved a fatal handicap. With the original Type 15 the design was much too complex and it became competitive far too late. The 2½ litre Type 25 was produced two years after a Formula had begun, and was not winning races until a year later. The 1½ litre Type 57 car was a year behind, but as Coventry-Climax were just as late this did not matter. The Type 83 H16 was back to the old problem of trying to crack a nut with a sledge hammer; it was persisted with so long that the V12 was introduced too late. With the Type 153, BRM attempted to catch up and, if the car had been more reliable, they might well have done so. It did, however, pave the way for the much more successful Type 160.

01 After a dreadful year when Jack Oliver failed to finish nearly all his races, BRM were long overdue for a new model and this duly arrived in time for the 1970 South African Grand Prix. In fact, two cars were ready, the first of which was to be Oliver's. The designer of the chassis was Tony Southgate, who had previously had a hand in the design of the Formula 1 Eagle, while the engine, originally designed by Johnson, had been modified by Aubrey Woods, from the Weslake fold, Harry Mundy and Wally Hassan, formerly with Coventry-Climax. The chassis followed Lotus practice and had the half monocoque with the engine forming the rear part of the chassis. The suspension was likewise standard but, for BRM, the car was very low and squat, resembling a pattern for the well-known Dunlop 'Groundhog' advertisement. But it looked a much better tool than the old Type 138 and 139 cars. The modifications to the engine mostly involved the cylinder head where the valves were relocated with inlet valves in the Vee and exhaust valves laterally. When the cars first appeared, the half shafts were constructed of tube which proved to be a mistake as two broke while Oliver was in practice for the South African GP, and special internally strengthened ones had to be flown out. Another problem was with the great heat in the cockpit; this was overcome to a certain extent by relocating the water pipes outside. In the race, the car showed

initial promise. Oliver was even in second place for one corner, but was soon in trouble when the car kept jumping out of gear, and this eventually caused his retirement.

By the time the Race of Champions was run, BRM had fitted more specially strengthened half shafts but, after leading for eight laps, Oliver suffered another breakage and had to retire. Incidentally this was the first time in the long history of the BRM team entry that the cars were not painted green. They were a sort of ivory colour with a brown and gold 'Y' on the bonnet, as the team was now sponsored by the Yardley cosmetic firm.

BRM had machined some new solid half shafts for the Spanish GP, but in practice Oliver broke a front stub axle and, when another failed in the race, he careered out of control across the inside of the hairpin and ran into the side of Ickx's Ferrari. Both cars crashed in flames and were destroyed, but luckily the drivers escaped virtually unhurt.

02 The second driver signed by the team was the dynamic Mexican, Pedro Rodriguez, an excellent choice as he could always be relied upon to have a go. His new car was also completed in time for the South African GP, but was delayed early on by misfiring, a fault which was cured by changing the ignition box. Rodriguez then had a trouble-free drive, finishing ninth. As BRM made only one entry for the Race of Champions, Rodriguez's next appearance was at the Spanish GP where he was stopped by his pit crew after Oliver's crash, and advised to retire because of the likelihood that the accident had been caused by faulty stub axles.

A gap before the next race allowed time for the front suspension to be redesigned and no further trouble was experienced with stub axles breaking. This time the problem was the ignition and, during practice for the Monaco GP, the initial system was replaced by Marelli ignition. In the race, Rodriguez had a stop early on with a sticking throttle, but this was repaired and thereafter he drove excellently, finishing sixth.

For the Belgian GP the rear suspension had been strengthened and the cylinder liners changed, as oil was being sucked into the combustion chambers. In spite of the gearbox playing up, Rodriguez drove a superb race; taking an early lead, he went on to a fine win. This was the first BRM success for four long years and was justly celebrated.

It was a shame that the car did not have a longer life, for it obviously suited Rodriguez. Sadly, he crashed it in practice for the Dutch GP and, although he was unhurt, the car was a write-off.

03 Luckily for the drivers, BRM had laid down a short series of cars and the third appeared in time for the Spanish GP, where it was practised by Oliver and broke yet another stub axle, fortunately without doing any damage. This car was now handed over for the rest of the 1970 season to the BRM No 3 driver, the Canadian George Eaton. He was never what might be called a star driver, but he had obviously gathered together enough money to finance a season's racing and, although he sometimes had difficulty in qualifying to start, he certainly enjoyed himself. An entry was made for him at the Monaco GP—surely, as far as Grand Prix racing goes, this was being thrown in at the deep end and predictably he failed to qualify for the start.

He was not entered for the high-speed Belgian GP, but in his next entry, the Dutch GP, the car did qualify to start. As regards development, 03 tended to lag behind the first two team cars, and for the race it was not fitted, as the others were, with titanium springs and Koni shock absorbers. It proved an unsatisfactory beginning for Eaton, as he ran in last position and retired early on with a loose oil tank.

For the French GP, the oil tanks were all modified to prevent surge, which had been a problem especially with the faster drivers. Also the tyres were fixed to the rim with four pegs instead of two—following an incident in practice for the Dutch GP when Rodriguez lost a tyre. After an early stop to have a loose plug lead replaced, Eaton soldiered on, driving quite well and, despite a further stop for a new wheel, when he had tried a little too hard and hit a barrier, he eventually finished twelfth.

A series of low placings and retirements followed for Eaton. The car was sometimes used as a guinea pig—for instance, in Austria a new type of Lucas fuel injection was tried. Eaton's best placing was in Canada where, in his home Grand Prix, he finished tenth. He was not invited to the Mexican GP, so his last race for the team for a long while was the United States GP, where his engine failed when he was lying twelfth.

The new Type 160 car was ready for the 1971 South African GP and this was driven by Rodriguez. BRM had now signed a new No 3 driver, Howden Ganley, who had many years' experience in Formula 3 and Formula 2; although this was his first foray into Formula 1, he proved to be a lot more competitive than Eaton but not, of course, in the top flight.

Ganley's first race was the South African GP where he was forced to retire physically exhausted, learning the hard way that Formula 1 is a lot more demanding than Formula 5000 in which he had raced the previous year. Luckily he had three minor races in which to acclimatise himself before the next big one and, with a fourth, a fifth and a seventh place to his credit, he could be proud of his baptism into the big-time.

After a tenth place in the Spanish GP, Ganley disgraced himself by colliding with Rollinson's Formula 5000 car in the International Trophy race at Silverstone. Although the BRM sustained no serious damage, it was to disappear from view for several months. It seemed that, after a long career, 03 had at last been laid to rest—as indeed it had, until the 1972 Argentine GP.

For 1972, BRM—allied with Marlboro cigarettes—determined on an enormous racing programme, entering as many as six cars in some races. This placed a great strain on the racing department and, when the new Type 180 was late to appear and then proved singularly unsuccessful, the 153s had to be resurrected for a while.

Reine Wisell, the Swedish driver, had joined the team and was given 03 for the Argentine GP. In Formula 3 Wisell and Peterson had thrilled the crowds with their duels, but when they came into Formula 1 Peterson forged ahead and Wisell never made the grade. It seems to be impossible to predict, from their success in lesser Formulae, which drivers will make their mark in Formula 1—unless, of course, they are of such rare genius as Fittipaldi or Stewart. Whereas Peterson remained the press-on-regardless driver he had always been, Wisell appeared easily discouraged and temperamental. He often declined what he thought to be non-competitive drives instead of making the best of a bad job. Peterson was to become the fastest driver in the world while Wisell's name is rarely heard.

In his first drive for BRM Wisell was unfortunate to suffer a sticking throttle followed by a water leak, so he had to retire. As only four cars could be taken to South Africa, Wisell was dropped from the line-up and his car acted as a spare for the

Austrian driver, Dr Helmut Marko, who had been with the team since the 1971 Italian GP. Marko showed tremendous promise and some correspondents likened him to the great Jochen Rindt in his early days—indeed, the two had been close friends.

The Brazilian GP was run for the first time in 1972 and so was of non-Championship status. For the race, 03 was loaned to the wealthy Alex Soler-Roig, who had been around for a long while in a variety of cars, all of which he drove fairly slowly; this occasion was no different and he retired with electrical trouble.

Marko was again in the driving seat for the Monaco GP, where the car was seen to be Type 153 as far as the rear of the cockpit and Type 160 from there to the end. As the front half was the chassis and carried the number, it was still technically 03. The weather was very wet for the race and Marko drove excellently to finish eighth. It was a great shame that his racing career was to be cut short so prematurely when his eye was badly injured by a flying stone in the French GP.

The factory was by now in a position to supply more of its reservoir of drivers with Type 160s, so 03 was finally retired from the scene after a long, long career.

04 As sometimes happens in Grand Prix racing, just when a factory thinks it has plenty of cars in reserve for its drivers to bash about, a series of setbacks occur so that the team is scratching round for machines for its eager beavers to drive. It was, therefore, fortunate that, when 01 was written off in the 1970 Spanish GP, 04 was nearly completed, and it was ready for Oliver in the next race, the Monaco GP. However, it had first to be fitted, like 02, with Marelli ignition, and it also suffered from gearbox trouble; these adjustments resulted in a loss of practice time and Oliver started from the rear of the grid. In the end this made little difference, as the engine blew up after forty-three laps.

After the race, the same modifications were made to 04 as had been carried out on 02 and 03, but Oliver was really going through engines at this time. One blew in practice for the Belgian GP and in the race he dropped a valve. It was the same story at Zandvoort where, after lying third, another engine blew, and at Auvergne, after blowing up another in practice, the replacement for the race

BRM 153/04   Now in its familiar Yardley cosmetic livery—Oliver drives the car in the British GP

went flat and Oliver retired; it was thought that some defect of timing caused the trouble.

In view of these engine problems, the oil circulation system was modified, as was the gearbox, but these changes had little effect. In the British and German GPs, Oliver suffered major engine failures, in spite of having a further modified oil tank fitted for the German race. However, perseverence prevailed and the problem was eventually cracked.

In the Austrian GP, despite a clutch failure, Oliver had a non-stop run to finish fifth for his first result since the 1969 Mexican GP. Just to show this was no fluke, he had a good ride in the non-Championship Gold Cup Race, even leading the second heat for a while; the suspension was set hard and he fell back a little, but still managed a fighting third place behind Surtees and Rindt.

Oliver's real triumph of the season was at the annual 'blind' round Monza. BRM would yield to no one as regards top speed and he made the most of his chance. What matter that eventually the engine went flat and he had to retire with overheating? He had led the world for ten laps, and that is something very few drivers—even after many years of trying—succeed in doing.

Sadly things were back to normal for the Canadian GP when a wishbone broke. The mechanics eventually replaced the offending part, but Oliver had too much ground to make up.

At the United States GP, Oliver deserted his faithful—well, perhaps not so faithful—car, and it was practised by Peter Westbury in his first and only sortie into Grand Prix racing. Having started off life driving an old Type 43 Cooper in a sprint at Snetterton in 1960, Westbury had graduated to hill climbs and won the British Hill Climb Championship. From there he went to Formula 3 and Formula 2, where he achieved further success, but he had left it a little too late to make the final step into Formula 1 and, when the BRM's engine failed in practice, Westbury never tried again.

Oliver was reunited with his car in Mexico and again finished, this time with an uneventful drive into seventh place. It was the end of the road for both car and driver, however; 04 had had a rough season and it was deemed to be surplus to requirements for 1971, so it was sold off. At the same time the team decided to replace Oliver with the Swiss driver, Jo Siffert. While there is no doubt that Siffert was very quick—not for nothing was he known as 'the last of the late brakers'—it may be thought that Oliver was one of several drivers who have been given a rough deal throughout their careers. One feels that Trevor Taylor, Peter Arundell and Chris Amon might all have gone far if they had had the right breaks, whereas Henri Pescarolo, John Miles and Joakim Bonnier, who had their chances, could make little of them in Grand Prix racing. Jack Oliver was certainly among the former—after all, as soon as he was put in the Lotus 49 he led the British GP, and no one can say fairer than that. However, at least he finally made his own little niche with the Shadow team on the CanAm scene.

05   As with 01, so it was with 02—when Rodriguez destroyed his first car in practice for the Dutch GP, he could step straight into 05 which had been newly finished for him. He nearly disgraced himself a second time when, in practice, a tyre came off the rim, but he averted an accident and the wheels were quickly modified. In the race the car went very well and Rodriguez rose as high as fourth place before having to stop for a loose cone to be replaced, which dropped him to tenth at the end.

Like Oliver, Rodriguez began to suffer the engine kick, having to get one changed in practice for the French GP. This was no help, though, as the car stuck in fourth gear and he had to retire from the race.

For sheer knockabout farce, the British GP took a lot of beating, although the mechanics would certainly have used a different phrase to describe it. The fun started when Rodriguez blew up in the first practice session. The engine was changed in time for the second session, but after two laps that blew up too. There was an unofficial practice session in the afternoon, for which the mechanics managed to replace the engine—and that one blew up as well! The race was not quite so dramatic perhaps, as Rodriguez merely suffered from severe wheel vibration so that eventually he just understeered gently off the road into the bank at Druid's hairpin. What a race! It was not surprising that, when the new 06 was unveiled for the German GP, Rodriguez preferred to drive it.

For the Austrian GP, he was back in the hot seat of 05; following an engine change, Rodriguez at last had an uneventful race and finished in fourth place.

It was back to the old problems in the Italian GP, when Rodriguez suffered a major blow-up, but at least he had the consolation of leading the race. The troubles with the engines were solved at last and, in the American series, Rodriguez had a much easier ride, though here a different snag arose: he twice ran out of fuel due to excessive consumption or insufficient tank capacity. This was a sad blow, as he was third in Canada and first in the United States at the time, yet he still managed to finish with a fourth and a second respectively.

The Mexican GP, where he retired with overheating, was the last occasion on which Rodriguez was to drive a Type 153. He remained in the team, but as its leader he was always given a Type 160 for his races. In Rodriguez and Siffert BRM had a team to beat all comers, but it was not to last for long. Tragically, little Pedro was to lose his life in a crash—not in a Formula 1 race, but in a tin-pot event at the Norisring. What a waste!

Like 04, 05 was found to be surplus to requirements at the end of the season, with the Type 160 coming along, and it too was never seen in Formula 1 again.

06   The factory managed to increase its stock of cars still further when it completed 06 in time for the 1970 German GP. Like 03—and indeed 07—this car was to have a long career. As Rodriguez was experiencing so many problems with 05, he decided to drive the new car in the race—it was the one after his treble engine change—but he had to give up because of ignition failure. After this, 06 became a practice and spare car until the American series of races, when Oliver used it in preference to his normal car, but suffered an engine failure in the United States GP. In the Mexican GP, 06 got to the finishing line in seventh place.

Although a Type 160 car had been completed for Rodriguez in time for the South African GP, Siffert's was not yet ready and he had to be content with the Type 153. He did not get far in the race as the car was overheating and nothing could be done to cure it. Before being transferred to his new car, Siffert used the 153 once more; this was in the Rothman's Trophy at Oulton Park where he suffered a puncture at the start, followed by ignition trouble which caused his eventual retirement.

The car now seemed set for a quiet life, but Ganley crashed 03 at Silverstone and, though it was not badly damaged, he transferred his flag to 06. Not surprisingly, he failed to qualify to start at Monte Carlo, but this was followed by good places in several races during the rest of the season. He had only one retirement, when a gear linkage failed at the German GP. This was Ganley's first appearance at the 14-mile Nurburgring and he distinguished himself by walking round the course in under five hours. The highlights of the year were in the non-Championship Rhein-Pokalrennen and Gold Cup Race, where a fourth and a second place were gained. As far as the World Championship series is concerned, the British GP was the best achievement as Ganley climbed up to fifth place before a puncture dropped him to eighth at the end.

Following the Gold Cup Race, Ganley was at last given a Type 160, and 06 remained in wraps until 1972 when, owing to the large size of the team. it was dusted off again. Marko was given the car for the Argentine GP, where he had a trouble-free race into tenth place, following this up with a fourteenth place in the South African GP. There were now sufficient of the more modern cars to go round, so the 153 was not seen again until the Gold Cup Race, when BRM made three entries and brought three different models to compete. The baby of the team, Vern Schuppan, was given 06 for his first race and drove sensibly enough to claim fourth place. After this showing. he was promised a drive in the Belgian GP but, when one of the 160s was damaged, Marko took over 06 from Schuppan and drove it to a steady tenth place. This was the last appearance in Formula 1 guise for this faithful old retainer.

07 At the same time that the new Type 160 was unveiled, the last of the Type 153s made its first appearance. It was tested by Rodriguez for the 1971 South African GP, but not used in the race, so that its first competitive showing was the Race of Champions when ex-team Lotus driver John Miles took it into seventh place after a tyre change. Miles used the car again in the Rhein-Pokalrennen when a retirement was posted with engine trouble.

After this, 07 was not used again until late in the season when Marko joined the team at the Austrian GP. He immediately impressed and finished eleventh; he would perhaps have been higher if he had not had to slow down towards the end with a collapsed wheel bearing. Having had early ignition failure at Monza, Marko again reached the finish with 07 in Canada, after which it was loaned to the staunch Formula 5000 supporter, John Cannon, for the United States GP. As a driver, Cannon is reminiscent of Ganley—not·of the highest order but always around and threatening if anything should go wrong for the front runners. In the race he finished fourteenth—and this proved to be the last appearance of 07 in competition for the major Formula.

The story of the Type 153 BRM is a sad one in many ways, for it was a good car, make no mistake about it. As has already been pointed out, if it had been produced even six months earlier it would have been a race winner. As it was, in 1970—as was shown by Rodriguez in the car's solitary win and by both Rodriguez and Oliver at Monza when leading the race—the 153 could, on its day, move really fast. What a pity this was not backed up by reliability in the engine department. Such unreliability in a particular department often shows up in the way a driver treats his cars. If, in spite of being driven comparatively carefully; a car keeps retiring with mechanical failure, the driver will say, in effect, 'Damn it' and drive it as fast as he can until it expires in a cloud of steam and smoke—which it probably would have done anyway. Naturally this can lead to a worse reliability record.

One good thing about the 153 was that it acted as the precursor for the Type 160—BRM's most successful car since the Type 57. The final memory of it is a sweet one, for no car that gave us the chance to watch Jo Siffert and Pedro Rodriguez at work can be all bad.

Results

Year and race	Chassis number and result						
1970	01	02	03	04	05	06	07
South African GP	Oliver R	Rodriguez 9					
Race of Champions	Oliver R						
Spanish GP	Oliver C	Rodriguez R	Eaton NQ				
Monaco GP		Rodriguez 6	Eaton NQ	Oliver R			
Belgian GP		Rodriguez 1		Oliver R			
Dutch GP		Rodriguez P/C	Eaton R	Oliver R	Rodriguez 10		
French GP			Eaton 12	Oliver R	Rodriguez R		
British GP			Eaton R	Oliver R	Rodriguez C		
German GP				Oliver R	Rodriguez P	Rodriguez R	
Austrian GP			Eaton P/C	Oliver 5	Rodriguez 4	Eaton 11	
						Rodriguez P	
Gold Cup Race				Oliver 3		Oliver P	
Italian GP			Eaton R	Oliver R	Rodriguez R	Rodriguez P	
Canadian GP			Eaton 10	Oliver 14	Rodriguez 4	Rodriguez P	
						Oliver P	
United States GP			Eaton R	Westbury NQ	Rodriguez 2	Oliver R	
Mexican GP			Rodriguez P		Rodriguez 6	Oliver 7	
1971							
South African GP			Ganley R			Siffert R	Rodriguez P
Race of Champions			Ganley 5				Miles 7
Questor GP			Ganley 7				
Rothmans Trophy			Ganley 4			Siffert R	

Results

Year and race	Chassis number and result						
	01	02	03	04	05	06	07
1971							
Spanish GP			Ganley 10				Rodriguez S
International Trophy			Ganley C				
Monaco GP						Ganley NQ	Rodriguez P
Rhein-Pokalrennen						Ganley 4	Miles R
Dutch GP						Ganley 7	
French GP						Ganley 10	
British GP						Ganley 8	
German GP						Ganley R	
Austrian GP							Marko 11
Gold Cup Race						Ganley 2	
Italian GP							Marko R
Canadian GP							Marko 12
United States GP							Cannon 14
1972							
Argentine GP			Wisell R			Marko 10	
South African GP			Marko S			Marko 14	
Brazil GP			Soler-Roig R				
Monaco GP			Marko 8				
Gold Cup Race						Schuppan 4	
Belgian GP						Marko 10	
						Schuppan P	

C=Crash; D=disqualified; NQ=non-qualifier; P=practice car only; R=retired; S=spare car not used

Cooper

Type 81

Type	81
Years of construction	1966-7
Number made	7
Frame designer	Derek White
Frame	Full-length aluminium monocoque with steel bulkheads and sides for engine bay. Suspension hung on bulkheads
Front suspension	Lower wishbone, upper rocker arm operating inboard coil spring/damper unit
Rear suspension	Lower wishbone, upper transverse link, two forward running radius arms with outboard coil spring/damper units
Engine make	Maserati
Engine designer	Sig Alfiéri
Engine type	10
Engine capacity	2989cc
Cylinders	12 in 60° Vee formation
Bore and stroke	70.4mm x 64.00mm
Valves per cylinder	1 inlet per cylinder in Vee, 1 exhaust per cylinder laterally (More powerful engine in 1967 had 2 inlet valves per cylinder)
Carburation	Lucas port fuel injection
Ignition	Lucas OPUS system
Sparking plugs	2 centrally placed 10mm plugs per cylinder
Camshafts per cylinder bank	2 overhead
Gearbox	ZF DS25 (in 1967 gradual switch to Hewland DG300—see text)
Brakes	Front inboard discs; Rear outboard discs

Cooper 81/F1-5-66   In its original shape—Bonnier achieves his best result with the car in the 1966 International Trophy

The Cooper Car Company had, by 1966, a long and honourable history in Grand Prix racing. Starting with Formula 3 in 1947, they had made a succession of highly successful small, rear-engined racing cars. Entering Formula 2 in 1952 with the front-engined Cooper-Bristol, they returned to the rear-engined layout for the new 1957 Formula 2 and used the same design for their first Formula 1 effort in 1958. The result was spectacular, for not only did they win the World Championship in 1959 and 1960 but they also transformed the Grand Prix world. In 1958 the Cooper was the only rear-engined Grand Prix car but, by 1961, only the sporadically appearing Ferguson was front-engined.

In the 1½ litre Formula, Cooper seemed to lose their impetus and built a succession of cars which were rather too heavy to be competitive. Unfortunately the same fault was to follow them into the 3 litre era. Coopers were plagued by the same obsession that affected several manufacturers—that power would be the only consideration—forgetting that the weight of the car was a vital factor. Cooper's answer was the Maserati V12 engine which first saw the light of day back in 1957 when Jean Behra used it in the gorgeous 250/F1 Maserati. It was then used in Maserati sports cars, to return to single-seater racing in 1966. This proved a fateful move for Cooper because the engine was very heavy and, while it is relatively easy to lighten a chassis, there is no way in which an engine can be made appreciably lighter.

F1-2-66 In 1965 Cooper constructed a space-framed car to take the Coventry-Climax 16-cylinder engine. This engine never arrived and the car was fitted with the Maserati engine to become the 1966 prototype. Hence it was numbered F1-1-66, although it was a Type 80 and not an 81; this explains why the first car in the 81 series was F1-2-66. It was made for a team financed by that long-established supporter of racing, R. R. C. (Rob) Walker, together with a newcomer, the wealthy stock-broker Jack Durlacher. The Walker team continued to use as their driver the popular and quick Swiss, Joseph Siffert. The F1-2-66 was ready for the first race in Europe to the new Formula at Syracuse, and it was interesting to note the new rivetted aluminium monocoque; despite this, the car was well over 100kg above the minimum weight limit. It must have been a sad blow to all Cooper followers when in practice the car was two seconds slower than the leading Ferrari. The race was not much better for,

after oiling the plugs at the start, a drive shaft broke and that was that. The International Trophy race at Silverstone saw the only race appearance of the Type 80, as Siffert broke the engine in F1-2-66 in practice and was loaned F1-1-66 only to retire with clutch failure.

It took quite a while for the engine to be replaced and although the car was at Monaco there was no engine to put in it, so Siffert had to race an old Brabham. The engine was repaired by the time the Belgian GP was held, but Siffert became involved in the mêlée halfway round the first lap. The trouble was that the weather was dry at the start, but unbeknown to the drivers torrential rain was pouring down at the far side of the course. It all began when Bonnier spun in his Cooper and demolished a wall. Spence crashed trying to avoid Bonnier, and Siffert while braking was rammed by Hulme. Sufficient damage was done to cause Siffert's retirement, although a head gasket had gone anyway. Hill, Stewart and Bondurant crashed independently, but in the same place, while Rindt had an enormous spin in front of Brabham, revolving at least six times without hitting anything and indeed without losing his second place.

F1-2-66 was easily repaired and appeared at the French GP. The main problem now was the engine, which ran very hot. This caused retirement at Rheims with fuel vapourisation; delay at Brands Hatch with internal maladies, and retirement at Zandvoort after a stop to refill with water. Following this, the car did not go to the German GP as Rob Walker had a different idea from that of the organisers as to the amount of money it should receive for starting. The problem of the engine was therefore not finally solved until Monza, where it blew up! Just as the team thought the season would end on a depressing note a minor triumph was achieved at Watkins Glen, where Siffert drove right through the field to claim fourth place and the first respectable result of the year. In Mexico, it was back to normal when a ball joint broke and a wheel was nearly lost.

Engine trouble reared its ugly head in South Africa, luckily for the last time, and the car celebrated its return to England with a good third in the Race of Champions. Now in its second season, the car began to be affected by a general slight unreliability; this is common with cars belonging to private owners, who presumably cannot afford new models as soon as the works teams can, and have to soldier on with outdated machinery. Although

Siffert had two third and two fourth places to show at the end of the season, it was still rather unsatisfactory because no sooner would one problem be corrected than another occurred—the car understeered at Zandvoort; the battery went flat at Le Mans; the throttle link stuck and a water pipe split at the Nurburgring; a starter ring broke in Canada, and a camshaft seized after an oil pipe split in Mexico. All these were minor troubles, though indicative that the car was at the end of its useful life. After a seventh place in the 1968 South African GP, the car was replaced by a brand new Lotus 49 and fresh glories for Siffert. As for the poor old Cooper, it was sold to the Swiss firm of Cegga and converted to Group 6 (sports car) regulations, and was even exhibited at the famous Geneva Motor Show.

Fl-3-66   The first of the factory cars appeared, in common with two others, for the first time in the 1966 International Trophy at Silverstone. While Jack Brabham was stroking his way home to victory, the Cooper—driven by the exciting Austrian prospect, Jochen Rindt—was having problems, mainly with the handling. This had been improved by Monaco, where Rindt showed that the car could be competitive by getting to third place before the engine blew up. Rindt's greatest day was at Spa where, after the monumental spin in pouring rain, he caught up with Surtees and overtook him in a masterly piece of driving. Unfortunately the ZF limited slip differential failed; while this did not really matter in the wet, it was too much of a handicap when the rain stopped, and Rindt was caught and passed by Surtees, nevertheless coming in a gallant second.

In common with most other Coopers that went fast enough, Rindt's car had problems with fuel vapourisation at Rheims, but finished fourth. Similar good placings followed in the British, German and Italian GPs, but the Cooper book was smudged by a failed gear change at Zandvoort, which caused the car to crash very early in the race. After a grand second place in the United States GP—where Rindt ran out of fuel on the last lap—the season ended on a sour note: at the Mexican GP a wheel was nearly lost when a ball joint broke.

Rindt was getting the placings, but was not fast enough to be right at the front. This was purely a result of the massive engine. At Monza an attempt had been made to partly solve the problem by inclining the inlet ports more inward, so that the engine would

be more compact, but the outcome was not startling.

In South Africa a further modification was used, the factory cars having Magneti-Marelli coil ignition, but this proved of little help when Rindt's car blew up. From Kyalami the cars were at last able to return to England where some intensive effort could be made to lighten them. Fl-3-66 appeared at Brands Hatch with a Hewland DG300 gearbox, much lighter than the original ZF variety; also inboard rear brakes were fitted. Rindt elected to drive the newer car, F1-1-67, in the Race of Champions, so F1-3-66 was raced in the heats by Ligier who had crashed his own car in practice. Ligier was classified fifteenth in heat 2, despite having suffered from clutch trouble. Rindt had been similarly affected in heat 2, albeit to a worse degree, and he decided to use F1-3-66 in the final, but was forced to retire with a recurrence of the clutch problem.

By the time Monaco came round, the engine and transmission from F1-3-66 had been transferred to F1-1-67 so that F1-3-66 could be fitted with the new, more powerful engine. This had three valves per cylinder—two inlet and one exhaust—and two plugs per cylinder as well. The result was an extra 30 BHP bringing the power output up to 380 BHP. There was never any intention to race the car at this stage, but it was thoroughly tested in practice by both Rindt and the other Cooper driver, Pedro Rodriguez.

As new cars were produced by the factory, F1-3-66 faded into the background as factory spare and general hack—for instance, Siffert practised it at Spa when his own gearbox failed. The car's last appearance was at the British GP when Alan Rees was given a 'one-off' drive and had a steady run to ninth place.

F1-4-66   Guy Ligier emerged from a not particularly distinguished career in Formula 2 when he purchased a brand-new Cooper for the 1966 Formula 1 season. The car was ready for the start of the season and he raced at Syracuse in company with Siffert. Unfortunately Ligier had a long pit-stop early in the race—with what turned out to be only a loose ignition pick-up lead—after which he plugged on to sixth place. Ligier seemed to specialise in unique problems: at Silverstone the engine scavenge pump failed—to my knowledge the only time this has occurred in a Cooper-Maserati—and he was therefore unable to start.

The Monaco GP was a shambles as a severe epidemic of

broken drive shafts hit the Coopers. Luckily, by the time Ligier's went, Rindt had retired and one of his was used so that Ligier could press on to sixth place, although he was too far behind to be classified and claim a World Championship point. There was a similar occurrence in Belgium where Ligier avoided the pile-ups but suffered clutch malfunction and again lost too much ground to be classified. The situation was to improve, however, as the bugs were shaken out, and Ligier officially finished the next three races.

Sadly these were the last occasions when the car was to appear in anger. At the German GP, Ligier spun off the road almost at the start of his first practice lap. He fractured a patella but soon recovered, while the poor car was wrecked beyond repair. Its engine later found a new home in Ligier's replacement, F1-7-66.

F1-5-66 By the time Joakim Bonnier came to purchase his Type 81 Cooper, he was a long way from being the brilliant driver who had carried BRM to their first Grand Epreuve victory. By now racegoers were used to seeing Bonnier towards the tail of the grid and often retiring on what seemed the flimsiest of excuses. This was a great shame because on those occasions when the spark reignited he could still turn in a rapid drive. Perhaps those present at Silverstone on F1-5-66's first appearance thought that 'Bearded Jo' was in for a new lease of life because Bonnier had a splendid drive into third place and shamed all the other Cooper drivers. But it was back to the rear of the grid at Monaco, with several pit stops caused by fuel starvation; and at Spa it was Bonnier who started the ball rolling with his crash at Burnenville.

As the car demolished a wall, it was a little while before F1-5-66 could be repaired and its next appearance was not until the Dutch GP, where Bonnier had a steady drive into seventh place. This was followed by several retirements before Jo got his first Championship points for some time when he finished sixth at Mexico City.

The car was retained for 1967 and taken to South Africa where a valve spring broke early in the race. When the clutch also failed, Bonnier retired. After retiring also from the International Trophy, with a split fuel tank, Bonnier gave the Monaco GP a miss, realising that he had little hope of qualifying to start the race. Instead he went to Syracuse where he was rewarded with a fifth

place. Two more retirements followed and it was thought that Bonnier was back to his usual style until he staggered everyone with a magnificent fifth place in that most difficult of all races, the German GP. This was a splendid achievement from a privately owned Cooper in its second year of racing and more than made up for all the disappointments.

Bonnier gained another point at Watkins Glen when he managed sixth place after a stop to change a wheel; and this was followed by a tenth place at Mexico City. The car's racing career drew to a most interesting end at Kyalami where it was involved in an incident without parallel in modern Grand Prix racing. Bonnier lost a wheel out on the circuit. Normally he would have retired, but on this occasion he retrieved the wheel and was able to refit it while a crowd of marshals lifted the corner of the car clear of the ground. He carried on, only to retire with overheating, which was not surprising!

This car is still in good order and residing in Derbyshire in the magnificent Donington Collection. The main interest of this collection is not so much in the rarities, such as the four-wheel-drive cars, but in those which had a long and honest racing career—including this Cooper, the Type 48 BRM and the true enthusiast's favourite, Godin de Beaufort's dear old fatty Porsche.

F1-6-66 Cooper had problems in 1966 with their No 2 driver to Rindt. For the first part of the season they signed Ritchie Ginther, who was only available until the new Grand Prix Honda was ready. Owing to an improperly made connection, a water cap came loose in the International Trophy causing the car to overheat and Ginther was forced to retire. In the Monaco GP, Ginther in common with Bonnier broke a drive shaft and the other of Rindt's half shafts was fitted, but unfortunately this failed as well.

After a slow drive to fifth place in the Belgian GP, Ginther left the team to go to Japan and Cooper could not have been more fortunate in their replacement. The vacancy happened to arise just as Ferrari, inexplicably, decided to dispense with the services of one of the very few really competitive drivers in Grand Prix racing at the time, John Surtees. As far as Cooper were con-

Cooper 81 B/F1-1-67 By now outdated but still trying—Rindt does his best in the 1967 French GP

cerned it must have been like finding Valhalla in their backyard. At the time there was no better tester and sorter of an evil car than Surtees and within a very few months he was to transform the car, for a short while, into a potential race winner.

Surtees showed his class in practice for the French GP when he performed a crafty move with Rindt to get hooked up with the very quick Ferraris of Parkes and Bandini, setting the third fastest time as a result. This proved of little consequence, however, as Surtees was the first member of the Cooper fuel vapourisation club and retired almost at the start of the race. Another retirement in the British GP led to Surtees changing cars for the Dutch, but he was back in F1-6-66 at the Nurburgring and a fighting drive into second place—Cooper's best result to date. Considering the clutch had packed up earlier, it was a superb effort, and even better was to come in his final two drives for Cooper before he moved across to try to sort out the Hondas.

At Watkins Glen, Surtees had an unfortunate bump when Arundell, whom he was lapping, got in his way. He lost a total of three laps having the car checked for damage, but drove splendidly and caught up two of these to finish in a marvellous third place. The climax was Mexico for here Surtees really drove it home when he claimed pole position on the grid. He led for almost the whole race to gain a memorable victory for the Cooper team—one which was almost as popular with the other teams as it was in the Cooper camp.

It must have been with some regret that Cooper said farewell to Surtees, but the sadness did not last long because they managed to obtain the services of that grand little driver, Pedro Rodriguez, who celebrated his arrival with a victory in the South African GP. This was much more of a win by default than Mexico for Pedro was headed at one time by John Love's four-cylinder Cooper-Climax, but a fuel stop gave Rodriguez the race.

Rodriguez kept to F1-6-66 for the greater part of the season and had some good results, only retiring from the Dutch and Belgian GPs with gearbox trouble. At Spa the same problem caused Rodriguez to miss a gear and the engine went bang. Eventually the car was fitted with a Hewland DG300 gearbox, the last factory car to have this done. The Type 86 cars were now the ones to use and, after a couple of retirements, F1-6-66 was sold to Mitsubishi of Japan, since when it has never been seen on this side of the globe.

F1-7-66 The last of the factory cars appeared at the 1966 French GP where it was driven by Chris Amon. That year he was No 2 driver for Bruce McLaren, who had a job to get even one car competitive, so that Amon had a slack season and picked up drives where he could. This one was better than most, as he finished eighth after stopping to have a wheel nut tightened. The car then became the factory spare. Surtees drove it in the Dutch GP, only to retire, but this was its final race of the year. The car was sold to Ligier at the beginning of 1967 to replace F1-4-66, but he had only three races with it for he crashed it in practice for the Race of Champions and had to borrow a factory car. After retiring from the International Trophy; finishing tenth in the Belgian GP and seventh in the French GP, after a stop to have the throttle linkage repaired, Ligier gave up the struggle and bought a Brabham instead.

The car was eventually sold to Jo Bonnier who prepared it for Andrea de Adamich to race in the Italian GP, but the arrangements fell through at the last minute and the car never appeared in Formula 1 again.

F1-1-67 For 1967 Cooper were preparing a new, much lighter and lower car, to be known as the Type 86, but this was not ready initially and, as an interim, they produced the Type 81B. Similar in many ways to the older cars, F1-1-67 was improved as regards weight with certain other detail modifications. For the present it retained the ZF gearbox. In the heats for the Race of Champions, the car was used by Rindt who hoped that the extra power from the new cylinder head would enable him to score, but the clutch failed and he was unable to drive it in the final.

The engine from F1-3-66 was inserted into F1-1-67 for the Monaco GP, but for some reason the Hewland gearbox had been temporarily discarded in favour of the usual ZF one. This would not fit properly and in the race caused Rindt's retirement when the bell housing came off the mountings. At the Dutch GP the Hewland gearbox was back in use, this time for good. Rindt got up as high as second in this race, but had to retire with handling problems. He achieved a fourth at Spa, always one of Rindt's best circuits. After retiring in the French GP, the car was not used in the next two races.

When Rodriguez was badly injured in a Formula 2 accident at Pergusa, Richard Attwood was signed to drive for Cooper in the

Canadian GP, but he showed little promise in finishing tenth. As a result Jackie Ickx, one of the Tyrrell Formula 2 stars, was signed for a couple of races, being rewarded with a sixth place in the Italian GP. Rodriguez was fit again for his last race with Cooper (he was leaving to join BRM) and in his native Mexican GP finished a very tired sixth.

Rodriguez was replaced in the team by Brian Redman, the popular driver better known for his work in big sports cars than Formula 1. Redman was not really given a chance with Coopers and retired in his only race with the Type 81, when the car overheated. After that it was all Type 86s with BRM engines.

The car was sold to hill climb specialist Martin Brain and was fitted with an American engine, which prolonged its career for several years.

And so the Type 81 Cooper-Maserati fades slowly into the west. Maybe it was not the most successful car of all time. Maybe it was a bit slow. Maybe it was heavy. But the big old Cooper generated the sort of affection that only a great, spectacular, hairy car can do. In this respect it had a certain amount in common with the beloved Lago-Talbots. It is a strange thing that cars like this tend to breed their own type of driver, which can be divided into two sorts—the wild and hairy 'last-of-the-late-braker' type and the slow plodder at the end of the field thoroughly enjoying himself. Just as Lago-Talbot had Etancelin, Sommer and Duncan Hamilton in the first category so Cooper had Rindt and Rodriguez; and just as Talbot had their Giraud-Cabantous and even Rosier so Cooper had their Bonnier and Ligier. Regrettably, the big, slow cars do not win money and Cooper's decision to go for the Maserati engine was the beginning of the end because, although a change was made to BRM power at the start of 1968, it was too late. The confidence of the top drivers had been lost. Stagnation had set in and it was but a year before one of the greatest names in the whole history of motor racing disappeared into obscurity.

Results

Year and race	Chassis number and result						
1966	F1-2-66	F1-3-66	F1-4-66	F1-5-66	F1-6-66	F1-7-66	F1-1-67
Syracuse GP	Siffert R		Ligier 6				
International Trophy	Siffert P	Rindt 5	Ligier NS	Bonnier 3	Ginther R		
Monaco GP		Rindt R	Ligier 6	Bonnier 7	Ginther 5		
Belgian GP	Siffert C	Rindt 2	Ligier 6	Bonnier C	Ginther 5		
French GP	Siffert R	Rindt 4	Ligier 9		Surtees R	Amon 8	
British GP	Siffert 12	Rindt 5	Ligier 10		Surtees R	Rindt P	
Dutch GP	Siffert R	Rindt C	Ligier 9	Bonnier 7	Surtees P	Surtees R	
						Rindt P	
German GP		Rindt 3	Ligier P/C	Bonnier R	Surtees 2	Surtees S	
Italian GP	Siffert R	Rindt 4		Bonnier R	Surtees R		
		Siffert P					
United States GP	Siffert 4	Rindt 2		Bonnier 11	Surtees 3		
Mexican GP	Siffert R	Rindt R		Bonnier 6	Surtees 1	Solana R	
1967							
South African GP	Siffert R	Rindt R		Bonnier R	Rodriguez 1		
Race of Champions	Siffert 3	Rindt (final) R			Rodriguez 4	Ligier P	Rindt (Ht2) R
		Ligier (Ht2) 15					
International Trophy	Siffert 3			Bonnier R		Ligier R	
Monaco GP	Siffert R	Rindt P			Rodriguez 5		Rindt R
		Rodriguez P					
Syracuse GP	Siffert 3			Bonnier 5			
Dutch GP	Siffert 10	Rindt S			Rodriguez R		Rindt R

Results

Year and race	Chassis number and result						
1967	F1-2-66	F1-3-66	F1-4-66	F1-5-66	F1-6-66	F1-7-66	F1-1-67
Belgian GP	Siffert 7	Siffert P		Bonnier R	Rodriguez 9	Ligier 10	Rindt 4
French GP	Siffert 4	Rindt S			Rodriguez 6	Ligier 7	Rindt R
British GP	Siffert R	Rees 9		Bonnier R	Rodriguez 5		Rindt P
German GP	Siffert 9			Bonnier 5	Rodriguez 8		Rindt P
Canadian GP	Siffert P			Bonnier 8	Rindt R		Attwood 10
							Rindt P
Italian GP	Siffert R			Bonnier R		Adamich P	Ickx 6
							Rindt P
United States GP	Siffert 4			Bonnier 6			Ickx R
							Rindt P
Mexican GP	Siffert 12			Bonnier 10			Rodriguez 6
1968							
South African GP	Siffert 7			Bonnier R			Redman R

C=Crash; D=disqualified; NQ=non-qualifier; P=practice car only; R=retired; S=spare car not used

Eagle

Types 1F and 1G

Type	1G
Years of construction	1966-7
Number made	4 (including one Type 1F chassis with Coventry-Climax FPF 2.7 litre engine)
Frame designer	Len Terry
Frame	Full-length riveted aluminium monocoque chassis with subframe for front and rear suspension
Front suspension	Lower wishbone, upper rocker arm operating inboard coil spring/damper units
Rear suspension	Double struts, two forward running radius arms, outboard coil spring/damper units
Engine make	Harry Weslake Engineering Ltd.
Engine designer	Aubrey Woods and Harry Weslake
Engine type	Gurney-Weslake 58
Engine capacity	2997cc
Cylinders	12 in 60° Vee formation
Bore and stroke	72.8mm x 60.3mm
Valves per cylinder	2 inlet per cylinder in Vee, 2 exhaust per cylinder laterally
Carburation	Lucas port fuel injection
Ignition	Lucas OPUS system
Sparking plugs	1 centrally placed per cylinder
Camshafts per bank	2 overhead
Gearbox	Hewland DG300
Brakes	Outboard discs

Eagle 1G/104   In its final form and shortly to admit defeat—Gurney's car in the pits at the 1968 British GP

When Dan Gurney left the Brabham team at the end of 1965 the firm of Anglo-American Racers had already been formed for nearly two years. At first the concentration had been on the building of cars to conform with the American single-seater Formula which, in effect, meant Indianapolis cars. In years to come a great deal of success was to come Gurney's way in this class of racing, but he resolved to enter Grand Prix racing in 1966 as well. Not content with his firm designing and building the car, Anglo-American Racers were also closely involved with the construction of the engine, for Gurney was the only driver-turned-constructor who was not going to use a proprietary engine. It was a brave decision and everyone waited to see whether Gurney could outshine Ferrari—or for that matter Hitler—by waging a war on two fronts.

Type 1F 101 The prompt appearance of the new Brabham in 1966 blinded motor racing enthusiasts to the fact that it is quite normal for constructors to take upwards of a year before producing their new effort at the start of a Formula. Gurney was no exception and, at the beginning of 1966, the engine was by no means ready and he appeared at the Belgian GP with an interim effort to keep his hand in. The chassis, as expected, was virtually identical to the Indianapolis car and impressed all by its workmanship, especially with regard to the riveting, which showed up sharply against the car's dark blue colour. Gurney was forced to use a four-cylinder Coventry-Climax FPF engine of 2.7 litres capacity. These were fine engines in their day, but the youngest was now at least four years old and so not entirely satisfactory. The gearbox was the one which was rapidly becoming standard wear in the Formula at this early stage—the Hewland HD5. A similarity was drawn by some people when comparing this car to the Lotus 38, an Indianapolis car, which was not surprising as Len Terry had a hand in designing each of them.

A second car had been entered for the race, but it never appeared throughout the season and the American Jerry Grant never did get to drive a Grand Prix car. As expected on such a fast circuit 101 was fairly slow in practice. The race was the scene of that famous crash sequence related in the previous chapter, but Gurney, with a sick engine, was going too slowly to be involved. He pottered along and eventually finished in seventh place, but he had not covered enough ground to be classified.

When the car appeared at Rheims it had been slightly modified by angling the rear arm of the front wishbone to give a better steering lock. Presumably Gurney must have had trouble negotiating La Source hairpin at Spa and foresaw similar problems at Thillois on the Rheims circuit. Steering dampers had also been fitted. Again Gurney had little hope of finishing in the money with his low-powered engine and, in fact, finished three laps behind the leader. However, this was sufficient to gain fifth place and two Championship points, as all the favourites dropped out.

When the team arrived at Brands Hatch the change in attitude was apparent for here they really had a fighting chance on the curves and bumps of Kent. Gurney staggered the regulars with a superb effort in practice which resulted in a place on the front row of the grid. This must have made all those behind with full 3 litre cars weep with frustration. In the race Gurney started well in second place, but shortly dropped to third. He held this position until, on the ninth lap, the poor old engine could take no more and broke a piston. At Zandvoort Gurney was again well up, holding sixth place till a head gasket blew. This was really only the final straw because a rear anti-roll bar had snapped and the oil feed pipe to the rocker cover had broken.

The best effort of all was at the Nurburgring where Gurney held fourth place until the very last lap when the engine stopped; a bracket securing the alternator had snapped, resulting in complete electrical failure. Hard luck indeed.

The car now became the second string, because the first of the twelve-cylinder cars was ready for the Italian GP. This was another fast circuit and Phil Hill, who was driving 101, failed to lap it fast enough to be allowed to start in the race. The car was taken across for the American series, but Hill was not well enough to drive and his place for the United States GP was taken by Bob Bondurant. Forced on to the grass at the start, Bondurant was unfortunately push-started by some marshals and this, of course, caused his disqualification. But 101 was still going quite well and, after having problems with the new car in practice for Mexico, Gurney took over 101 for the race and had a trouble-free ride into fifth place.

The new car was now nearly competitive, so 101 was used by the factory on only one more occasion—the 1967 South African GP. Gurney got as high as third before a left rear wishbone broke, causing his retirement from a race which he would undoubtedly have won had he kept going. The car, now surplus to requirements, was sold off complete to three Toronto enthusiasts, one of whom was driver Al Pease. Unfortunately, at the Canadian GP he was unable to start the car and lost fifteen minutes and a large number of laps while having the battery replaced. Pease entered the Canadian GP in both 1968 and 1969 with 101, thus ensuring that, as well as being the first Eagle to appear in Grand Prix racing, it was also the last. On neither occasion was triumph the result: in 1968 Pease failed to start after engine trouble in practice, while in 1969 he was disqualified for being too slow—surely the ultimate indignity. The car now resides in the Donington Park racing car museum.

Type 1G 102 Like 101, the new car impressed all who inspected it at the 1966 Italian GP with its superb workmanship. The chassis was already well known, the only change from 101 being the simple wishbones in place of the braced ones. But it was the engine that really impressed, particularly by being far the most compact V12 ever seen. Developed by V12 expert Aubrey Woods at Harry Weslake's engineering works, this was a 60° engine with each bank having twin overhead camshafts in a single camcover. The single plug per cylinder was central throughout the cam cover. The inlet valves were in the Vee with the exhaust valves placed laterally. As over 300 BHP were obtained at the first running of the engine, the car was rushed to the Italian GP but, both in practice and in the race, gross fuel feed problems were encountered. These were no sooner overcome than the oil temperature started to rise; so, before this could create a serious hazard to the engine, the car was retired.

This problem was solved by the time the car arrived in America but was replaced by low oil pressure; in addition, a fuel cell had to be changed when it split in practice for the United States GP. Nevertheless, the car definitely showed promise and was one of the quickest on the timed straight. In the race there were again fuel problems when the metering unit played up, as did the ignition system. In spite of these faults Gurney struggled up to eighth place only to develop severe clutch slip owing to oil leaking on to the plates; this eventually caused his retirement. Gurney now realised that, if his personal position was not to be affected, he would have to sacrifice the car's undoubted speed

for some reliability; so Bondurant drove 102 in Mexico, and it was not taken to South Africa, in order that development could proceed apace. Incidentally, Gurney's decision was proved correct as Bondurant failed to finish in Mexico—that old bogey, fuel vapourisation, caused by the heat and the altitude, intervened.

The Eagles are being discussed here in a little more detail than the other cars because, having only a short history, it is instructive to see what problems a manufacturer comes across and how he tries to solve them. At this stage the trouble was mainly with the fuel system. Gurney saw that by returning from Mexico direct to England, and missing out South Africa, the team would have five months in which to sort out the problems and construct new cars before the next World Championship race at Monaco. Also, in March, there was a convenient race at Brands Hatch, the team's local circuit, where the cars could be race tested. In addition, the impetus would not be lost as it is when teams are forced to miss races in mid-season.

The Race of Champions at Brands Hatch proved how well the team had solved their problems when they simply walked over the opposition. Gurney had signed the experienced Ritchie Ginther as his No 2 and they fitted together perfectly. In practice, Gurney was over a second faster than anyone else—a tremendous margin in modern Grand Prix racing—and, on the day, he won each of the heats and the final, leading each from start to finish. The only time he was approached was right at the end; Bandini in the new Ferrari nearly caught him when Gurney was slowing with falling oil pressure.

Gurney appeared in the same car in practice at Monaco, but swopped with Ginther as 103 had a smoother working throttle linkage. Ginther sadly failed to qualify 102 in spite of trying as hard as he could. As he also failed to qualify for Indianapolis he became very dispirited and decided to retire from racing. This was a great shame because Ginther, always a popular driver, had shown he was as quick as anyone at Brands Hatch.

For the time being Gurney had to soldier on by himself; then he was joined for the French GP by Bruce McLaren who was in a worse position than Gurney with his cars. McLaren was given 102 and, in return, gave the mechanics an overnight job with an engine change when the oil scavenge pump driving gear failed. The second engine was not as powerful, due to the rather strange drive to the ignition which sheared, causing it to slip and gradually retard the ignition until it was so bad that McLaren had to retire. At the British GP, the mechanics had to struggle again when a con rod let go at the end of practice, necessitating another engine change, and the same thing happened in the race when McLaren was lying seventh.

It was another sad story in the German GP where the car bottomed badly round the 'Ring and, when an oil scavenge pipe was fractured, McLaren had to retire, this time with an intact engine.

Compared with the new car, 104, 102 was quite heavy and, as Gurney had decided on a solo effort in 1968, the car was retired after one more race. As McLaren had now got his own car into something like working order, Lodovico Scarfiotti was co-opted for the Italian GP. A previous race winner, Scarfiotti was not so lucky this time; the scavenge pump housing broke and damaged the timing gear after only six laps of 102's last race. The car was bought by Scuderia Filipinetti for Herman Müller to drive, but never raced because of the non-availability of a suitable engine.

Type 1G 103

When Ginther joined the team in 1967 his car was fitted with a specially shaped aluminium seat set very well forward because Ginther is one of the shortest, if not *the* shortest Grand Prix driver of all, being barely 5ft tall. This had proved an advantage in the previous Formula, when power was the only consideration, and it was calculated that a man of his size would need about 3-4 less BHP to propel him at the same speed as Gurney. At Brands Hatch, while not quite as dominating as Gurney, Ginther nevertheless did his bit. Third in the first heat, split by Surtees, and second in the second heat, Ginther ran second to Gurney in the final until the car started to feel 'funny' and, rather than risk a brand new car in a minor race, Ginther retired. It was later found that the only trouble was a lost balance weight from one wheel.

The car was taken over by Gurney for the Monaco GP after the first practice session and he took with him the suspension from 102. For the race, both cars were modified with special bumper bars at both ends to minimise damage in the start-line scramble. It all came to naught, however, as 103's fuel injection pump belt broke early in the race. The car made one further appearance—in Canada. In 1967 the Canadian GP was held before the Italian GP, so that to cover all the races some cars had to cross the Atlantic

four times. To avoid having to do this, 103 was fitted with the titanium suspension and other bits from 104, and taken to Canada. In practice the fuel injection metering unit broke, and when this happened a second time it was decided to change the engine. At last everything held together and despite two stops for fresh goggles—it was pouring with rain—Gurney finished a good third. The car was bought in 1969 by Danny Ongais for the American Formula A races.

Type 1G 104

Whereas the previous three cars had all been fairly similar, the fourth departed radically from the pattern, not in its geometry but in the materials used in its construction. When 104 appeared for the 1967 Dutch GP, the other mechanics were, quite frankly, staggered. The constructors had used a large amount of titanium and magnesium for strength with lightness. Titanium is notoriously difficult to weld, but the quality of the welding was superb, so that the car was immaculate and a real credit to Anglo-American Racers. The car was 100lb lighter than the existing models and it was no surprise when Gurney put the car on to the front row of the grid. He was third away at the start, but the early promise was not maintained, as the fuel mixture was playing up again, and the metering unit finally gave out on lap 9.

By now the team must have been feeling a bit frustrated. They knew the cars were quick but they could not get them to the end of a race. All was forgiven at Spa, however, when Gurney was again on the front row; in spite of a slow start and a brief stop to complain of low fuel pressure, he came through strongly to take the lead from Stewart on lap 21, and stormed on to win by over a minute. Here at last was the just reward for all their efforts.

In France, it was back to normal when Gurney was running second. This time it was a broken union in the injection unit, due to a high frequency vibration, which caused his retirement. Before the British GP the titanium front rocker arms were replaced by steel ones which it was hoped would be more rigid. The brakes were off form here, however, and from an initial sixth place Gurney gradually lost touch with a slipping clutch and soon had to retire. The German GP was particularly sad. Taking the lead on lap 4, Gurney led easily until, with only two

Eagle 1G/103   A rare picture of Scarfiotti in practice for the 1967 Italian GP. It was his only drive in the car

and a half laps to go, a drive shaft universal joint broke, cutting through an oil pipe in its flailings.

There was a little time to spare before the Italian GP, with 103 being taken to Canada, and new sheet steel hub carriers were made, while much detail lightening and strengthening was carried out. Yet again 104 flattered only to deceive and, after leading on the first lap, a con rod broke on lap 5 and that was that. It was a similar story in the United States GP, where Gurney again held an initial second place, but after eight laps the pin holding the lower rear wishbone to the upright broke.

At Mexico, not surprisingly, there were new rear uprights and a new engine, but when Clark's Lotus hesitated at the start who was just behind? Yes, poor old 'Dan, the driving Man'! An exhaust pipe from the Lotus punctured the radiator and Gurney only lasted three laps.

Although there was plenty of time before the 1968 South African GP, the only evidence of improvement in the car were new exhaust pipes and even these were replaced with the old ones for the race. At Kyalami, as at Mexico, there is usually a fuel vapourisation problem caused by the altitude, and Gurney ruined two fuel pumps in practice and started the race with refrigerated fuel. At least this time the car survived more than ten laps and climbed to seventh place, but he had to give up after fifty-seven laps with an oil leak. Monaco proved to be the worst yet. The team were running an engine made completely by them—as opposed to Weslake—with new pistons and rods, but it blew up almost at the start of practice. The replacement arrived late and Gurney was at the back of the grid. Not that this made much difference, for he only lasted nine laps and then, with overheating, ignition trouble and an intermittently functioning fuel pump, the car collapsed into the pits.

By now the firm was at rock bottom. They had given their all and it was still not enough. Success in America was proving far easier to achieve; first and second places were gained in the Indianapolis 500. The Formula 1 effort was gradually run down and only three more races were entered before Gurney resigned and drove in Canada for McLaren, the Eagle being no longer competitive.

These last three races were a catalogue of failure. For the British GP, a redesigned fuel system (not before time), new con rods, wider wheels and aerofoils had been fitted, but the fuel pump failed at the start and Gurney only completed eight laps. The German GP was the most successful of the year; after a puncture, a ninth place was salvaged. The final straw was the Italian GP, where the car failed to show anywhere near the right end of the queue and overheated its way into history after nineteen laps. The car is now on display at the Cunningham museum in California, USA.

Few cars have gone from such promise to such failure in so short a time as the Eagle did in Grand Prix racing. From a first place in Belgium 1967—seen by everyone as Eagle's take-off point after which all the others would be struggling—it was less than a year to the back of the grid at Monaco. The reasons are not difficult to find, the most important being that the reverse had happened in the United States where, from upstart intruders, the team had gone through to win at Indianapolis. We have already seen the difficulty of trying to do two things at once, and Gurney attempted as a small firm to make his own engine. This was a mistake. The results showed, particularly by recurring faults, that the engine was not getting the development it needed from a specialist firm, such as Weslake. No small firm (always excepting Ferrari) has made a success of engine manufacture owing to the expense and expertise necessary to be successful at the highest level of the sport. It has always been left to the specialists to provide the best engines. If the team had left Weslake in charge of engine development, the outcome might well have been different. The engine was basically a good one and, to this day, the occasional rumour circulates about its reappearance. For the experts still feel in their heart of hearts that a good 3-litre V12 should be able to beat a good 3-litre V8.

Results

Year and race	Chassis number and result			
1966	1F/101	1G/102	1G/103	1G/104
Belgian GP	Gurney 7			
French GP	Gurney 5			
British GP	Gurney R			
Dutch GP	Gurney R			
German GP	Gurney 7			
Italian GP	Hill NQ	Gurney R		
United States GP	Bondurant D	Gurney R		
Mexican GP	Gurney 5	Bondurant R		
	Bondurant P	Gurney P		
1967				
South African GP	Gurney R			
Race of Champions		Gurney 1	Ginther R/10	
Monaco GP		Gurney R	Ginther NQ	
Dutch GP		S	S	Gurney R
Belgian GP		S		Gurney 1
French GP		McLaren R		Gurney R
British GP		McLaren R		Gurney R
German GP		McLaren R		Gurney R
Canadian GP	Pease 14		Gurney 3	
Italian GP			Scarfiotti R	Gurney R
United States GP				Gurney R
Mexican GP				Gurney R

Results

Year and race	Chassis number and result			
1968	1F/101	1G/102	1G/103	1G/104
South African GP				Gurney R
Monaco GP				Gurney R
British GP				Gurney R
German GP				Gurney 9
Italian GP				Gurney R
Canadian GP	Pease P			
1969				
Canadian GP	Pease D			

C=Crash; D=disqualified; NQ=non-qualifier; P=practice car only; R=retired; S=spare car not used

Ferrari

Type 312

Note cylinder heads modified as follows:

(1) 0001 onwards—inlet valves between camshafts, exhaust valves in Vee
(2) 0007 onwards—2 inlet valves per cylinder laterally, 2 exhaust valves per cylinder in Vee
Single sparking plug per cylinder
(3) 0017 onwards—2 inlet valves per cylinder in Vee, 2 exhaust valves per cylinder laterally

Type	312
Years of construction	1966-9
Number made	12
Frame designer	S.E.F.A.C. Ferrari S.p.a.
Frame	Steel tube space frame with riveted, stress-bearing panels modified in later models to full monocoque chassis
Front suspension	Lower wishbone, upper rocker arm operating inboard coil spring/damper units
Rear suspension	Lower wishbone, upper transverse link, two forward running radius arms with outboard coil spring/damper units
Engine make	Ferrari
Engine designer	S.E.F.A.C. Ferrari S.p.a.
Engine type	312
Engine capacity	2991cc
Cylinders	12 in 90° Vee formation
Bore and stroke	77.0mm x 53.5mm
Valves per cylinder	1 inlet per cylinder in Vee, 1 exhaust per cylinder laterally
Carburation	Fuel injection
Ignition	Coil and distributor
Sparking plugs	2 centrally placed plugs per cylinder
Camshafts per bank	2 overhead
Gearbox	Ferrari 312
Brakes	Outboard discs

When the new Formula was announced, it was automatically assumed that Ferrari would be among the front runners. After all, he always had been since way before the war when he used to race the official Alfa-Romeos under the banner of Scuderia Ferrari. The team had struggled during the 1½ litre Formula, but still had two World Championships to show for their pains. They had a ready-made engine in the sports car 3-litre V12 engine and the chassis compared favourably with other cars in the last year of the previous Formula. Therefore it was with eager anticipation that everyone waited for the 1966 Syracuse GP and the unveiling of the new car. Initially they were not disappointed, but gradually things went wrong and, as far as Formula 1 racing goes, Ferrari did not recover until 1975.

010 At Syracuse, Ferrari really had everything going for them. They had ex-World Champion John Surtees, one of the finest driver/mechanics in the world, as No 1 driver and they had a competitive car all ready to go. The chassis followed standard Ferrari practice from the previous Formula, having a basic steel tube space frame with stress-bearing panels. The suspension was also the standard double-wishbone layout with coil springing. As expected, the engine was the 60° V12 with twin overhead camshafts, one plug and two valves per cylinder, with the inlet valves central in the Vee and exhaust valves laterally placed. It was no surprise when Surtees from pole position led almost from the start against—apart from the new Coopers—weak opposition. At Silverstone, however, when the car could not wrest pole position from Jack Brabham and in the race had to follow at a discreet distance, a few eyebrows were raised but nobody seriously thought Ferrari were going to be closely challenged for the Championship. Monaco, too, was no real indicator as Surtees was in the lead after twelve laps when the differential housing broke due to the stress put on it by the constant gear-changing and increased engine power.

Sure enough, Ferrari were back to their rightful position when, in the Belgian GP, Surtees at last passed Rindt after the rain stopped and won easily. Then, following a dispute with team manager Dragoni, Surtees left the team. This was absolutely

tragic, and quite why Enzo Ferrari should have allowed this to happen is beyond belief. How he could expect to carry on, even with the fastest car, is difficult to understand. Nevertheless, this was what he did, and Bandini, Parkes and Scarfiotti had to do their best.

At Rheims the effect was not noticeable for top speed was of paramount importance and from pole position Bandini led until a throttle cable snapped and the race was lost. At the British GP there were no Ferraris to be seen. One cannot imagine this situation happening if Surtees had still been with the team. At Zandvoort they reappeared with their cars sporting new rear suspension uprights and extra lugs so that the upper radius arms could be adjusted if necessary. But the impetus had been lost. Bandini crashed the car in practice and could do no better than sixth with the repaired but badly handling motor. A similar position was the sad result in Germany but, as always, Ferrari saved his best efforts for the annual spectacular at Monza.

The secret was the new engine fitted to all three cars. This differed mainly in having three valves per cylinder. There was one lateral exhaust valve as before, but the two inlet ports were both between the two camshafts. There were still two plugs per cylinder and the power output was greatly increased. The cars were very fast and Bandini led the way in 010 until a fuel pipe broke. After this was repaired, he helped Parkes and Scarfiotti in the slipstreaming battle until ignition failure caused his retirement.

In the United States GP, 010 again led for a while until, it is thought, part of a sparking plug dropped into a cylinder and caused an engine blow-up.

As usual Ferrari constructed a new batch of cars for the 1967 season and 010 appeared only once more—in the practice sessions for the Race of Champions at Brands Hatch, when Chris Amon drove it. However, he had sustained some injuries in a road accident and was unable to start in the race. The car therefore returned to the factory and was presumably broken up, as was standard Ferrari practice when a car reached the end of its useful life.

011 This was originally intended to be Bandini's car, but plans were changed when Surtees left the team. In 1966 Bandini had used 011 in practice at Monte Carlo and Spa, preferring to race the old V6 car until he was quite confident of his ability to handle

Ferrari 312/010 Watched by Surtees and Forghieri, the mechanics adjust the car before the 1966 International Trophy the more powerful V12. When he found himself No 1 driver, he naturally took over the car on which all the development work had been carried out by Surtees. This left 011 in the wilderness and it did not see a Grand Prix circuit again until Monza when it reappeared, with the new engine installed, for Scarfiotti to drive. He excelled himself and, when Bandini stopped at the pits, Scarfotti took over the mantle of team leader, coming home to a fine win after an excellent fight with the Brabham team.

In 1967 the car was used three times before the new series took over completely. Scarfiotti finished fifth in the Race of Champions and then—in spite of 011 still having the Monza-type engine, as opposed to the new one which Bandini introduced at the Race of Champions—he finished first, equal with Parkes, in the Syracuse GP. The car's final appearance was as a spare for Scarfiotti in the Dutch GP.

012 The third car in the first series was one all on its own as it was built for the very tall Michael Parkes. He had long been known in England for his skill in saloon and grand touring cars, and this was his first serious attempt at Formula 1 racing, although in the distant past he had driven the old Formula Junior Geminis. To accommodate Parkes' great height the car had more length in the cockpit area and an extended frontal portion, but in other respects was much as before.

Parkes handled the car for the first time at Rheims in the French GP, when he did really well to finish second to Brabham. He had been appointed chief test driver at Ferrari and obviously had not wasted his time. In the Dutch GP, however, he blotted his copybook when he missed a gear change and crashed the car. There was a similar occurrence in Germany when, during a spell of misfiring, 012 left the road and parked itself among the trees. Luckily there was time to spare before the Italian GP for the car to be fitted, like the others, with the modified engine. Parkes, like Scarfiotti, was involved in the struggle at the front but, helped by Bandini when he rejoined the race, came through to finish second.

This was the last race in which Parkes took part in 1966. When the car reappeared as a lone entry for the International Trophy, it had the new engine which Bandini had used in 0001 at Brands Hatch. It was obviously powerful enough, for Parkes had no difficulty in winning the race on a circuit which he knew very well indeed. After a steady drive into fifth place at Zandvoort Parkes terminated the car's racing career with a crash during the Belgian GP. Although he only sustained a fractured leg, it was three years before he raced again. The car was thoroughly destroyed.

0001 The first car in the 1967 series was basically similar to the 1966 cars, although it had higher pontoons at the rear to accommodate the narrower engine and hold more fuel. The engine was the big difference—while the configuration was basically the same, even to the extent of the inlet ports still being between the camshafts, the exhaust pipe had been moved into the centre of the Vee. There was a complicated system of exhaust pipes now above instead of to the side of the engine. That the car was good was proved by Bandini when he just failed to catch Gurney on the finishing line of the Race of Champions in a grand race.

Bandini was carrying on the good work at Monaco with the same car in a fine second place behind Hulme, when he made a slight error of judgement. The car crashed, burst into flames and was completely destroyed. Although Bandini was rescued alive from the blazing wreckage, he died from his injuries—and Italy lost her only Grand Prix driver of any stature.

0003 The second car of the new series had been completed in time for the Monaco GP and was driven by Amon. When Bandini crashed, he inherited second place, but a puncture dropped him to third. The car, virtually identical to 0001, was reliable from the outset, taking a fourth place in the Dutch GP and a third in the Belgian. However, doubts as to its speed were by now apparent, as Amon took a long time to dispose of the Cooper-Maseratis. Ferrari now entered a long, flat period.

Following the death of Bandini and the injury to Parkes, Scarfiotti lost interest in Formula 1 racing and returned to his first love, hill climbing. This left Amon on his own in the Formula 1 team and, with Ferrari attacking sports-car racing, their efforts in the single-seater sphere became somewhat diluted. It was not until the very end of the 1967 season that Ferrari made two entries in a race, when Jonathan Williams drove 0003 into eighth place in the Mexican GP. In between times Amon had used it mainly as a practice car, although he had a good third placing in the British GP.

At the start of 1968, Ferrari increased their Formula 1 effort by signing the young Jackie Ickx to partner Amon, but again their attack was not wholehearted for they were also attempting Formula 2 for the first time for many years. Nevertheless, the season was a little more successful than that of 1967.

Ickx began on an inauspicious note when he spun and crashed 0003 at the South African GP; he had, however, been in sixth place at the time. In common with the other cars, 0003 had been fitted with the new four-valve engine first seen in 0007 at Monza 1967.

In the Race of Champions, Ickx was forced to make a stop with fuel pump trouble, but finished eighth. By Ferrari standards the car was becoming somewhat long in the tooth and was not seen again until the Belgian GP, when Ickx managed a fine third place despite an engine which was only firing on eleven cylinders for the major part of the race. The car then seemed to fade into retirement, only to be dusted down for the American series, being used by Amon for practice purposes in Canada and the United States. It was actually raced in Mexico where Ickx drove it, but early on in the race the car suddenly stopped with a mysterious ignition complaint.

0005 After Bandini was killed, Scarfiotti was again drafted into the team and was provided with a new car. With this he managed a sixth place in the Dutch GP and, despite a stop with a broken hydraulic pipe to the rear brakes, an eleventh in the Belgian GP. This was the race in which Parkes had his accident and Scarfiotti withdrew from racing. Amon then took over 0005 as his main weapon and achieved some good results, with a fighting third in Germany as the pinnacle. The detailed race-to-race development, which is such a part of Grand Prix racing, was lacking at this stage and, when 0007 was produced at the Italian GP, 0005 was relegated to the background, being driven by the wealthy young, Andrea de Adamich, to a desultory ninth in the non-Championship Spanish GP. The car was fitted with the new engine for the South African GP, but de Adamich overdid things and crashed. He finally finished off 0005 when he crashed in practice for the Race of Champions.

0007 Just when everyone was thinking that Ferrari had collapsed into oblivion by making only one entry for the Italian GP, which

Amon was to drive, he produced a new car. Normally Ferrari raised his biggest effort of the season for the annual blind round Monza, having been known to enter as many as six cars, but things had changed. Nevertheless the new car was in many ways a great achievement. The chassis was similar to established practice, except that even more alloy was used to save weight, but it was mainly in the engine department that Ferrari moved away from his normal practice. The engine had a four-valve head with the two exhaust valves in the Vee and two inlet valves outside. Not only were the two sets of valves at a very narrow angle, but the inlet valves were slightly angled to each other, as were the exhaust valves, giving an approach to a radial valve layout. In fact, the engine showed a likeness to the Apfelbeck BMW engine, as was pointed out by Denis Jenkinson in *Motor Sport*. The narrow angle between the valves meant that there was no room for the ports between the camshafts, which were therefore covered by a common cam cover with the ports outside. The other major departure was to single plug ignition.

One would like to be able to say that the result was a first-time victory, but this was not to be; in the race the car was delayed by a faulty shock absorber and Amon only managed seventh place. The story was no better across the Atlantic when, in the United States GP, the engine blew owing to loss of oil pressure, but at least Amon had been in second place for a long while. In Mexico the unpardonable happened—when well up in the field, Amon ran out of fuel. The car was used throughout 1968 with few major modifications to show. This was the year of the aerofoil and, even in a car of rather bad design, the road-holding could be made passable by the simple means of fitting enormous wings. Eventually the matter got completely out of hand and, early in 1969, after bad accidents involving two Lotuses, the high-mounted wings were banned. In fairness, it must be said that Ferrari never went to such excess in this respect as other constructors; nevertheless the aerofoil evolution did tend to stultify other development.

Amon started off the year reasonably well with fourth places at Kyalami—in spite of a stop for fuel—and Brands Hatch. He improved on this in the International Trophy race with a good third, even though he had a fight with his spare goggles after his first pair broke. By the time of the Spanish GP, Amon was in fine form and it really looked as if he was going to achieve the long-awaited victory when he was well in the lead. Then the fuel pump packed up and that was that. After this, 0007 became Amon's practice car and it was not used again in a race until Derek Bell drove his first Formula 1 race for Ferrari in the Gold Cup at Oulton Park. He had a lot of trouble with the gearbox sticking in gear, and finally the engine blew up—a most unusual occurrence for Ferrari. Bell drove the car again in the United States GP, only to suffer another engine failure. Afterwards 0007 was taken away to a not untimely retirement.

0009 The car that Ickx was to use in the 1968 season was ready for him at the International Trophy meeting and, after Amon had checked to see that it was all right, Ickx drove it to a satisfactory fourth place. The car was very similar to 0007, but even more use had been made of light alloys in the construction of the frame. The result was the most successful Ferrari since the palmy days of early 1966. Its start was not promising for in the Spanish GP Ickx was forced to retire with ignition failure, but he was lucky in that there were several very wet Grand Prix races during 1968 which suited him down to the ground.

Ferrari gave Monaco a miss, after both cars had retired in Spain, and arrived at Zandvoort ready for action. Ickx quickly got down to business and finished a fine fourth in pouring rain. At Rouen for the French GP, the rain poured down from start to finish, but this did not worry Jackie. He took the lead at the start and stayed there right through the race to claim Ferrari's first win for over a year. This put Ickx's name on that very short list of Grand Prix *drivers*, as opposed to Grand Prix participants of which there are many.

Ickx followed this win with a third place in the British GP, but a new car had now been completed for him and 0009 had to take a back seat. Ickx used 0009 at Oulton Park when it suffered an ignition malady, and Bell drove it in the Italian GP, retiring early on with fuel feed trouble. It was taken to America as Amon's main car and showed a new lease of life in Canada, where again it looked as if Amon was going to win his first Grand Prix. However, he had been driving without a clutch for the whole race until the transmission finally stripped and he coasted into the pits for a sad retirement. The car never showed such form again, retiring from the other two transatlantic races.

In 1969, the car made two final appearances—Bell drove it to

an undistinguished ninth place in the International Trophy and later it was dusted off when Pedro Rodriguez started to drive for the team. Presumably Amon's contract said that he should have two cars available at each race, so 0009 was the only remaining Grand Prix Ferrari for Rodriguez to use. It was far from competitive, having been away from the fray for six months, and Rodriguez must have been pleased when, at Silverstone, the engine broke and he could retire to the pits.

0011 Amon's main challenge for the 1968 season made its appearance at the Belgian GP. The car was to have a short life but a violent one. Things started off promisingly enough with a struggle for the lead, but the usual Amon luck struck when the oil radiator was punctured by a stone and engines cannot run without oil. Amon at this time was convinced that he could not drive in the rain, and steady rather than quick races were the form in Holland and France. In Britain, however, he profited by other drivers' retirements and finished second to Siffert when he won his first Grand Epreuve.

It was wet again for the German GP, but by now Amon had come to terms with the rain and was up as a front runner when some form of transmission failure caused the car to start weaving about the track and, shortly after, to crash. It was repaired for the Gold Cup Race and, after losing time at the start, Amon had another fighting drive into second place, smashing the lap record in his pursuit of Stewart.

This period was arguably the pinnacle of Amon's career for in spite of a car which was basically three years old, he was always up at the front pitching in as hard as he could, and was desperately unlucky not to have been rewarded with a victory. Time and time again he would take the lead only to be delayed by some trifling fault. Nevertheless, 0011 was probably not to blame when it met its end in the Italian GP. Amon spun on a patch of oil, was hit by Surtees and smashed into the barriers, wrecking the car but fortunately not himself.

0015 The replacement for the tired 0007 appeared at the 1968 German GP, in the hands of Jackie Ickx. The plan was identical

Ferrari 312/017 Amon in preparation for the final season of the 312. By the time it raced, the car had a new nose section and the small front fins had disappeared

to 0011 and, in spite of spinning twice in the very wet conditions, he finished a creditable fourth. This was improved on at Monza where he held second place until the very end of the race, when vapour locking in the pipes caused intermittent cutting of the engine so that Servoz-Gavin was able to overtake him. Surprisingly this proved to be the last race for the unfortunate 0015 as, in practice for the Canadian GP, the throttle jammed open and Ickx piled into a bank, breaking a leg and wrecking the car.

Although it was not apparent at the time—for Ferrari's car movements have never been well documented—it is now obvious how stretched Ferrari must have been to provide competitive cars for Amon to drive in the remaining races in 1968. Any remarks about 'old nails' would certainly be justified but not for long, as there was a new car on the stocks.

0017 The cognoscenti were surprised when, in South Africa, the new car was seen to have a chassis identical to that of the 1968 cars. This was apparent when 0017 was even referred to in reports as 'last year's car'! What was new was the engine. Ferrari had decided to standardise as far as possible Formula 1 and prototype engine design, so the valves were reversed with the inlets now in the Vee and the exhausts laterally. Also the oil circulation system was completely revised. It was claimed that this gave an immediate power improvement to 436 BHP at 11,500 RPM. This may have been so, but sadly the power was not matched by reliability.

Although Amon managed a tenth place in the International Trophy meeting, after a stop to have the wing readjusted because the car was bottoming on the bumps, 0017 failed to finish in the first five Grand Prix in which it started. Engine trouble in South Africa, Spain (when leading) and France, plus a dismal showing in the British GP, caused Amon to refuse to race again for Ferrari until the new car was ready.

It will be apparent that development had been lacking for the past year on the 312 and the new car was the reason. It had long been rumoured that a 312B was on the way, with a flat 12 engine, and for the last half of 1969 Ferrari was just marking time with the old cars.

So it was that Pedro Rodriguez was given 0017 for the American series. The Canadian GP saw the fourth successive retirement of the car—again with an engine complaint, in spite of

having reverted to the 1968 type engine. This time the problem was oil pressure, or rather lack of it. The United States GP was a comparative triumph; in spite of a pit stop for a tyre change, Rodriguez managed to persuade the car across the finishing line in fifth place. This was not enough, however; after a slow seventh in Mexico, the Type 312 finally faded from view and it was not before time.

0019 The very last car of the series appeared at the 1969 Monaco GP, where it was driven by Amon, but the differential failed. It finished third in Holland after a grand race with Hulme; it was used a couple of times in practice, again by Amon, and finished sixth at Monza with Rodriguez driving—and that was that. The 312 appeared three times more—but that was 0017; 0019, after one of the shortest voluntary careers of all, had been relegated to the shelf.

Where had Ferrari gone wrong? The Formula had such a promising start, with the best driver, the best car, the best set-up and the biggest will to win—or so we all thought. Things began to go awry when Surtees departed and, even after all this time, it is still incredible that he was allowed to go. Enzo Ferrari knows very well that you can have the best cars in the world but, if you have not got the best drivers, you have no chance.

In 1962 Ferrari allowed his Formula 1 effort to be dissipated by simultaneous efforts in sports cars and prototypes. As a result several of his managers and engineers left his employ. Surely he should have learnt his lesson then. Nobody, except Mercedes-Benz, can mix *successful* Formula 1 and sports car racing. Ferrari discovered the truth of the above remark for the second time when he tried Formula 2 as well. If a firm is racing on so many fronts, the talents and developments are spread far too thinly.

Finally Ferrari waited far too long before accepting that the 312 was outdated. This was a fatal mistake because, by the time the 312B was produced, it was already trying to catch up rather than leading the way—as, say, the Lotus 72 did when it came out. The time lost by Ferrari in the late 1960s was of paramount importance because a month lost in Grand Prix racing takes a long, long while to catch up.

It took five long years before Ferrari caught up.

Results

Year and race	Chassis number and result					
1966	010	011	012	0001	0003	0005
Syracuse GP	Surtees 1					
International Trophy	Surtees 2					
Monaco GP	Surtees R	Bandini P				
Belgian GP	Surtees 1	Bandini P				
French GP	Bandini 10		Parkes 2			
Dutch GP	Bandini 6		Parkes C			
German GP	Bandini 6		Parkes R			
Italian GP	Bandini R	Scarfiotti 1	Parkes 2			
United States GP	Bandini R					
1967						
Race of Champions	Amon P	Scarfiotti 5		Bandini 2		
International Trophy			Parkes 1			
Monaco GP				Bandini C	Amon 3	
Syracuse GP		Scarfiotti 1=	Parkes 1=			
Dutch GP		Scarfiotti P	Parkes 5		Amon 4	Scarfiotti 6
Belgian GP			Parkes C		Amon 3	Scarfiotti 11
French GP					Amon P	Amon R
British GP					Amon 3	
German GP					Amon P	Amon 3
Canadian GP						Amon 6
Italian GP						Amon P
United States GP					Amon P	

Results

Year and race	Chassis number and result					
1967	010	011	012	0001	0003	0005
Mexican GP					Williams 8 Amon P	
Spanish GP						de Adamich 9
1968						
South African GP					Ickx R	de Adamich C
Race of Champions					Ickx 8	de Adamich P/C
International Trophy						
Spanish GP						
Belgian GP					Ickx 3	
Dutch GP						
French GP						
British GP						
German GP						
Gold Cup Race						
Italian GP						
Canadian GP					Amon P	
United States GP					Amon P	
Mexican GP					Ickx R	

Results

Year and race	Chassis number and result					
	0007	0009	0011	0015	0017	0019
1967						
Italian GP	Amon 7					
United States GP	Amon R					
Mexican GP	Amon 9					
Spanish GP						
1968						
South African GP	Amon 4					
Race of Champions	Amon 4					
International Trophy	Amon 3	Ickx 4				
		Amon P				
Spanish GP	Amon R	Ickx R				
Belgian GP	Amon R		Amon P			
Dutch GP	Amon P	Ickx 4	Amon 6			
French GP	Amon P	Ickx 1	Amon 10			
British GP	Amon P	Ickx 3	Amon 2			
German GP		Amon P	Amon C	Ickx 4		
Gold Cup Race	Bell R	Ickx R	Amon 2			
	Amon P					
Italian GP	Amon P	Bell R	Amon C	Ickx 3		
	Ickx P					
Canadian GP		Amon R		Ickx P/C		
United States GP	Bell R	Amon R				
Mexican GP	Amon P	Amon R				

Results

Year and race	Chassis number and result					
1969	0007	0009	0011	0015	0017	0019
South African GP					Amon R	
International Trophy		Bell 9			Amon 10	
Spanish GP					Amon R	
Monaco GP					Amon P	Amon R
Dutch GP					Amon P	Amon 3
French GP					Amon R	Amon P
British GP		Rodriguez R			Amon R	Amon P
Italian GP						Rodriguez 6
						Brambilla P
Canadian GP					Rodriguez R	
United States GP					Rodriguez 5	
Mexican GP					Rodriguez 7	

C=Crash ; D=disqualified ; NQ=non-qualifier ; P=practice car only ; R=retired ; S=spare car not used

Honda

RA273, RA300, RA301 and RA302

Type	RA273
Year of construction	1966
Number made	3
Frame designer	M. Sano
Frame	Full-length monocoque with pontoons at rear to support engine and suspension, sub-frame to support front suspension
Front suspension	Lower wishbone, upper rocker arm operating inboard coil spring/damper unit
Rear suspension	Lower wishbone, upper transverse link, two forward running radius arms with outboard coil spring/damper units
Engine make	Honda
Engine designer	M. Nakamura
Engine type	RA273
Engine capacity	2992cc
Cylinders	12 in 90° Vee formation
Bore and stroke	78.0mm x 52.2mm
Valves per cylinder	2 inlet per cylinder laterally, 2 exhaust per cylinder in Vee
Carburation	Honda port fuel injection
Ignition	Coil and distributor
Sparking plugs	1 centrally placed 12mm plug per cylinder
Camshafts per bank	2 overhead
Gearbox	Honda RA 273
Brakes	Outboard discs

Type	RA300
Year of construction	1967
Number made	1
Frame designer	Eric Broadley
Frame	Monocoque centre section with sub-frame for front suspension, tubular frame running from rear of monocoque underneath engine to rear bulkhead supporting rear suspension
Front suspension	Lower wishbone, upper rocker arm operating inboard coil spring/damper units
Rear suspension	Lower wishbone, upper transverse link, two forward running radius arms with outboard coil spring/damper units
Engine	as RA273
Gearbox	as RA273
Brakes	Outboard discs

Type	RA301
Year of construction	1968
Number made	2
Frame designer	M. Sano
Frame	Full-length aluminium monocoque with front and rear bulkheads to support front and rear suspension
Front suspension	Double wishbones with external coil spring/damper units
Rear suspension	Lower wishbone, upper transverse link, two forward running radius arms with external coil spring/damper units
Engine	as RA273
Gearbox	as RA273
Brakes	Outboard discs

Type	RA302
Year of construction	1968
Number made	2
Frame designer	M. Sano
Frame	Monocoque centre section with monocoque pontoon to rear from which are suspended the engine and gearbox. Pontoon supports upper rear suspension, gearbox supports lower rear suspension, forward bulkhead supports front suspension
Front suspension	Lower wishbone, upper rocker arm operating inboard coil spring/damper unit
Rear suspension	Lower wishbone, upper transverse link, two forward running radius arms with outboard coil spring/damper units
Engine make	Honda
Engine designer	M. Nakamura
Engine type	RA302
Engine capacity	2987cc
Cylinders	8 in 120° Vee formation, air-cooled
Bore and stroke	88.0mm x 61.4mm
Valves per cylinder	2 inlet per cylinder in Vee, 2 exhaust per cylinder laterally
Carburation	Honda port fuel injection
Ignition	Coil and 2 distributors
Sparking plugs	1 centrally placed per cylinder
Camshafts per bank	2 overhead
Gearbox	Honda RA302
Brakes	Outboard discs

Honda RA273/F-103   In the car's near final appearance, Surtees practises for the 1967 Italian GP—in the race he used the new 'Hondola', and won

51

The firm of Honda had for many years spearheaded the effort of the Japanese motor cycle industry in the World Motor Cycle Championships. They had done so not with faithful copies of Western machinery—as they were, according to myth, supposed to do; they produced machines that were original in every way, such as the 125cc five cylinder and the 250cc six cylinder, which were music to the enthusiast's ear. When it was announced that Honda were to enter the world of Grand Prix racing in 1964, the fans looked forward with anticipation to their first appearance. They were not disappointed in the twelve cylinder transverse engine layout which Bucknum and later Ginther campaigned. When Honda won the final race of the $1\frac{1}{2}$ litre Formula it was a very popular victory for Ginther.

Type RA273 F-101

Honda's first effort in the 3 litre Formula, when displayed for the first time at the 1966 Italian GP, was quite frankly a big disappointment. For one thing it was far too heavy—240Kg over the 500Kg limit, which no amount of horsepower could overcome. It was obvious almost from the start that Honda, like BRM, had attacked the problem from the wrong angle. In the all-consuming search for power the simple alternative—saving of weight—was ignored. This proved to be a fatal handicap and the car never won a race. The construction was orthodox monocoque but the engine was unusual in being a 90° V12 instead of the more normal 60° angle between the cylinder banks. All bearings were roller in type, which is all very well if they lead to an appreciable increase in power—as with the 1966 Formula 2 engine—but is not worth the increased weight if they do not. The engine layout reverted to normal compared with the $1\frac{1}{2}$ litre car when it was seen to be mounted longitudinally. The exhaust valves were in the Vee with the inlet ports between the camshafts. The plugs were central, being inserted between the inlet port and the exhaust valve camshaft.

Honda had appointed as their driver the number one from 1965, Ritchie Ginther, who was invaluable as a test driver and, on his day, as quick as anyone. The car only made the second row in practice, but was running in second place in the race when a rear tyre punctured and Ginther ran off the road into the trees, completely wrecking the car, although he himself only sustained a fractured clavicle.

Type RA273 F-102

The replacement for F-101 had a track measurement $7\frac{3}{4}$in wider to try to improve the poor road-holding. Ginther, recovered from his injury, raced the car, but had to have a pit stop when the transmission oil overheated and caused gearbox selection problems. By the time the cars arrived in Mexico an oil cooler had been fitted. Although the car was still running at the end of the United States GP it was too far behind to be officially classified. In Mexico it actually led for the first two laps but steadily lost ground, finishing fourth.

The car continued to be the mainspring of the team's effort in the major part of 1967. Honda, possibly even more than Cooper, benefited by Surtees' departure from Ferrari. When he signed for the team they gained one of the best testers and drivers in the world. Until the communications of the team between Japan and England became too stretched, Surtees dominated the situation and Honda were a force to be reckoned with.

At the beginning Surtees ran a race test programme on F-102 by entering it for three successive races and not changing anything major on the car from race to race. These were the South African GP, the Race of Champions and the Oulton Park Spring Trophy. Before South Africa various minor changes had been made—to the suspension in particular. Apart from a retirement in the Race of Champions, due to a sticking throttle; an intermittent ignition fault in the Spring Trophy and red-hot pedals in South Africa, the car ran very well albeit slowly and was rewarded with two third places.

After so much race mileage the car was rested at Monaco, being used as a mobile test car in practice by Surtees. It had not finished work yet, however, and was used right through to the German GP. With a sixth and a fourth place it might be thought that the car ran well, but this was not so. In the British and German GPs the engine sounded terrible, and the ignition kept cutting out as it had done right at the start of the season. In the Belgian GP Surtees suffered an enormous engine blow-up, breaking even the camshaft.

So it was with not too much regret that Surtees said farewell to F-102. It had served him for nearly a year, but whether it served him well is another matter.

Honda RA301/F-801   The Lola design Type 300 was soon modified by Honda, and here Surtees drives the modified car in the 1968 Spanish GP

Type RA273 F-103 When F-101 crashed at Monza it was lucky that two more cars were being finished for, in addition to Ritchie Ginther, Honda had contracted their 1964-5 driver, the American Ronnie Bucknum. This car did not have the wide track of F-102 but retained the narrower track of F-101. It made its first appearance in the United States GP, where Bucknum retired the car as the engine got rougher and rougher as successive exhaust pipes burnt away. Things got more personal in Mexico when a seat started burning, but luckily Bucknum was able to stop before any lasting damage was done to his anatomy. The electrical short circuit was corrected and Bucknum carried on to finish eighth—and last. The car was destined to have only one more race in its career; this was at Monaco early in 1967. Surtees preferred the car to his usual one but blew a head gasket as early as lap two and was forced to retire after thirty-one laps. So, although it was taken to all the races until Monza as back-up car for F-102, this proved to be the end of F-103's short career.

At this point in the middle of the 3 litre Honda history it might be instructive to indicate a singular facet in the Honda make-up. In almost all the organisation's models there seems to have been a total lack of development once the car set off on the circuits— the exact opposite of Lotus, in fact. Despite John Surtees' long research and development programme with the RA273 and the RA301, no major modification materialised. Similarly with the air-cooled car, after a couple of brief appearances it was never seen again. It is almost as if, once the car was made, Honda lost interest—in the same way that Alessandro de Tomaso, king of all dilletantes, used to do.

All through 1967 it was obvious that all was not well with the Honda in that most basic of departments—road-holding. That problem and the one of weight were solved in a brave and unusual way. It happened that Eric Broadley and his firm of Lola were very close to John Surtees' England base of the Honda enterprise. They had been closely associated before, so it was not surprising that Broadley was approached to design the replacement chassis for the RA273.

Type RA300/1 The result was predictable in so far as a great saving in the weight of the chassis was achieved, and remarkable in the fact that the project was completed in just six weeks.

The car was fitted with a new engine and gearbox, but these were basically the same as before. The difference was in the chassis which had a monocoque centre section made of riveted alloy sheet. The front suspension was hung on the forward bulkhead and the engine on the rear bulkhead. A tubular structure ran underneath the engine to another bulkhead which supported the rear suspension. This meant that the engine was not part of the chassis, as in the case of the Lotus 49, and is now de rigeur in Grand Prix racing. The 1967 Italian GP was a justification for all the work for, in spite of the fuel injection not being quite right, Surtees was well up all the way. When the Lotus 49s failed, he just beat Brabham to the line and so won on the car's first appearance.

By the United States GP the car had been fitted with stronger wishbones and the engine had been back to Japan but was still misfiring. When the metering unit broke, the one from the other engine was fitted. The race was a chronicle of misfortune. It started quite well when Surtees worked his way up to sixth, but then a piece of rubber got in the works and caused a misfire. After that was sorted out, an exhaust pipe broke and overheated the fuel metering unit so that Surtees had to stop twice to have it cooled. The final straw came at the end of the second pit stop when the car would not start due to a flat battery—the alternator had failed.

In view of the continuous problem with the fuel system, this was modified again for Mexico, where in spite of some differential trouble Surtees had a steady drive into fourth place.

It was thought at the time that this car would be Honda's weapon for the next season as it had been reasonably competitive, but already the first development model was being prepared in Japan. So RA300/1 had only one more race before being retired; this was in South Africa where Honda's decision to build a new car was justified. While the car was quite reliable it was now two seconds off the pace and could only finish in eighth place.

Type RA301 F-801 The car appeared at the 1968 Spanish GP for the first time and it was sad to see that Honda had gone back to their old ways. When the car was weighed it was found to be 90lb heavier than Broadley's Type RA300. The main modification was in the engine department so it must have been here that the weight was gained. The most startling sight was the new valve gear; this was based on the remarkably successful 1966 Formula 2 car that won all but one race for which it was entered. This latter car, incidentally, had a Brabham chassis with the Honda engine fitted.

The valve gear in this engine was activated by cams and closed by torsion bars, a most unusual solution to the problem. The inlet ports were placed in the Vee with the exhaust ports lateral to the cam covers. The engine now lay in a monocoque cradle as the part behind the engine had been increased in width and height. It must have been heartbreaking to find that the fuel-feed problem was still present. It is strange how a certain fault can dog a particular manufacturer for years without a solution being found—one recalls the San Remo Maseratis with their oil leak. The car was also handling badly but nevertheless managed to get up to third place, when part of the gear selector mechanism broke and fell into the gearbox. In Monaco, the gearbox broke again after a singularly fraught practice session, when the crown wheel and pinion stripped and the drive shaft universal joint broke.

Honda had always been happier at the faster circuits and it was good to see Surtees again as a front runner, leading the race until his rear suspension broke. The car was fitted with an aerofoil for the first time here. It is amazing to look back at 1968 and see what a wet season it was. Zandvoort was the first really damp race and, although alternator trouble was given as the cause of Surtees' retirement, the real reason was that the driver was fed up after several pit stops and a spin. What was the point?

Although the new V8 was ready for the French GP, Surtees did not consider the car to be competitive at that time and wished to carry out a long development programme on it. So he stuck with the V12 and was proved right for, although he had to stop quickly for a new pair of goggles—it was raining again—he finished a good second. The car continued on its steady way, the picture being enlivened in the British GP when the aerofoil fell off. Nevertheless Surtees managed a fifth place, which was better than the wet German GP where a retirement was posted this time with ignition trouble.

So Surtees was glad to be back to the wide open spaces and sure enough it was once more a battle for the lead. The Honda had led the Italian GP for a time until Amon spun on some oil in front of Surtees and the impact damage resulted in an unfor-tunate retirement. Not seriously damaged, the car was repaired so that it could retire twice and finish once in the American series of races. In the United States GP it achieved a third place with a fresh engine fitted. The retirements were in the Canadian GP, with gearbox trouble, and in the Mexican GP, the last Grand Prix in which Honda have competed to date, where the car only lasted eleven laps before the water pump broke and the engine overheated. It was said at the time that Honda were withdrawing from racing to consider their position. It certainly needed considering.

Type RA301 F-802 It is difficult to say why Honda produced a brand new machine when they were to retire from racing; perhaps, having completed the chassis as a spare, they felt they might as well give it a whirl instead of just leaving it in the garage. The chassis was constructed of aluminium and not, as F-801, largely of magnesium. Built at Slough in John Surtees' workshops, it was lighter but as strong as the original car; also the rear suspension had been slightly modified. The lucky driver chosen to pilot the car in the 1968 Italian GP was David Hobbs who even in those days had been around a while. He was one of those excellent sports-car and Formula 5000 drivers who for one reason or another—not necessarily lack of talent—never made the grade in Formula 1. He by no means disgraced himself in the race, for he got up as high as sixth before an unfortunate dropped valve caused his retirement.

The car was never to race again as Surtees used it as a training car in the United States. Nevertheless it was not just left to rot. In Canada it broke a wishbone and vapourised its fuel when it overheated. In the United States it was fitted with its Monza engine which had been back to Tokyo, but it would not rev properly. Also it broke a crown wheel and pinion. An attempt to cure the lack of revs was made before Mexico by changing the entire ignition system. But it was too late. Time had run out.

Type RA302 F-801 When the time came for the annual running of the French GP in 1968, rumours of a new Honda had been in the air for some while. These were confirmed when the car was tried out at Silverstone by Surtees. He did not think it was ready to race and was probably right, but matters were not quite as simple as that. Mr Honda himself was in France on a trade mission and both he and the race organisers wished the car to run. When Surtees refused, it was entrusted to the long-time supporter of Formula Junior and particularly Formula 2 where he was very popular—Jo Schlesser. It cannot have escaped notice that Schlesser was French, so the move to put him in the new car was naturally a popular one.

An inspection of the car in the paddock revealed that it was completely new and bore no resemblance to any previous Hondas, except in so far as it had an engine, gearbox and four wheels—in fact, it had very little resemblance to any previous Grand Prix car.

In describing the car it is probably easiest to consider the engine which proved to be an air-cooled V8. One tries hard to recall other air-cooled Grand Prix contenders and, after noting the Formula 1 Porsches of beloved memory, the mind becomes a blank. But those were flat-fours and flat-eights—the V8 was new. Cooling was by two large scoops at the side, and use was also made of the cooling effect of the oil by having a large oil tank and a high circulating rate. Mr Honda's idea of introducing air into the crankcase to cool the oil mist before being extracted did not work very well and was dispensed with in the second model. As regards the more normal side of the engine, it was a 120° V8 with four valves per cylinder, all worked by torsion bar springing. The inlet ports were in the Vee with the exhaust valves laterally outside the camshafts. A new five-speed gearbox was fitted. The chassis was monocoque with an extension over the engine—in the Vee, in fact, between the two rows of inlet ports—and the engine was suspended from this. The suspension was about the only bit that did not differ from standard practice. The result, at last, was a Honda that was right down on the Formula minimum weight limit.

One could not expect the car to conquer the world on its first appearance and it was quite slow in practice. Schlesser played himself in carefully, trying to get used to the tremendous increase in power under his right foot, compared with the Formula 2 McLaren.

Race day was very wet and all the drivers set off cautiously. The Honda was misfiring from the start and, on the way down through the curves to the Nouveau Monde hairpin, the engine cut completely. Schlesser spun off the road into the bank where the car overturned, caught fire and burnt out, poor Jo being killed instantly.

It may well have been this tragedy more than any other single factor that prompted Honda's withdrawal from racing at the end of the season.

Type RA302 F-802 Another of the 302 series, however, was eventually produced, at the Italian GP. Although it never raced, it was used in practice by Surtees but suffered from an oil leak which proved temporarily incurable. The car was almost identical to Schlesser's except that the air cooling of the oil in the crankcase had been abandoned. Cynical journalists of the time felt that, as Mr Honda had thought of the idea, it had to be incorporated, but the engineers also designed the engine so that it could operate without the crankcase cooling in case it did not work. The journalists were probably right!

So that was that. It is always a sad time when a firm withdraws from racing, especially when it is one of the big factory teams. But one can see Honda's point. By their success in motor racing, they had aimed to increase the sales of their road cars, and when this success proved hard to achieve they realised the futility of throwing good money after bad and packed it in.

In a world where the simple way of doing things is often the best, Honda seemed to look for more complicated ways. Unfortunately complexity usually weighs more than simplicity—as Honda found to their cost. With the exception of the RA302, their cars were always far too heavy which affected not only the straight line acceleration but also the road-holding. The number of extra horsepower Honda needed to equal, say, the Repco-Brabhams for performance must have been staggering. It boils down yet again to the importance of appreciating the crux of a Formula. In the early days the answer was not just power; although it helped, but adequate power with excellent road-holding and especially light weight.

It is interesting to see how the problem has changed over the years. Now the engines all turn out roughly the same power; the cars are all as light as they can be and are equipped with the same basic tyres etc. The answer lies in modification from race to race. New demon tweaks are soon spotted by the opposition and

Honda RA302/F-801   Seen at its release to the press, this exciting new model was to be completely destroyed in Schlesser's tragic accident a few days later

copied, but tuning the car for the individual circuit is of paramount importance. This is why, for instance, the wheel base of the M23 McLaren can be varied by inserting spacers between the engine and gearbox.

Today there is a vast difference from the big, heavy Hondas which thrilled the fans back in 1967. These cars had one attribute which the enthusiast will always remember above all else: they made a lovely noise—and that makes up for a lot.

Results

Year and race	Chassis number and result			
1966	RA273/F-101	RA273/F-102	RA273/F-103	RA300/1
Italian GP	Ginther C			
United States GP		Ginther 8	Bucknum 10	
Mexican GP		Ginther 4	Bucknum 8	
1967				
South African GP		Surtees 3		
Race of Champions		Surtees R		
Spring Trophy		Surtees 3		
Monaco GP		Surtees P	Surtees R	
Dutch GP		Surtees R	Surtees P	
Belgian GP		Surtees R	Surtees S	
British GP		Surtees 6		
German GP		Surtees 4		
Italian GP			Surtees P	Surtees 1
United States GP				Surtees R
Mexican GP				Surtees 4
1968				
South African GP				Surtees 8

Results

Year and race	Chassis number and result			
1968	RA301/F-801	RA301/F-802	RA302/F-801	RA302/F-802
Spanish GP	Surtees R			
Monaco GP	Surtees R			
Belgian GP	Surtees R			
Dutch GP	Surtees R			
French GP	Surtees 2		Schlesser C	
British GP	Surtees 5			
German GP	Surtees R			
Italian GP	Surtees C	Hobbs R		Surtees P
Canadian GP	Surtees R	Surtees P		
United States GP	Surtees 3	Surtees P		
Mexican GP	Surtees R	Bonnier 5		
		Surtees P		

C = Crash; D = disqualified; NQ = non-qualifier; P = practice car only; R = retired; S = spare car not used

March

721, 721X and 721G

Type	721
Year of construction	1972
Number made	4
Frame designer	Robin Herd
Frame	Monocoque centre section with subframe for front suspension, engine forms rear part of frame
Front suspension	Double wishbones with tubular rocker arms working inboard coil spring/damper units
Rear suspension	Lower wishbone, upper transverse link, two forward running radius arms with outboard coil spring/damper units
Engine make	Cosworth
Engine designer	Keith Duckworth with Mike Costin
Engine type	DFV
Engine capacity	2993cc
Cylinders	8 in 90° Vee formation
Bore and stroke	85.7mm x 64.8mm
Valves per cylinder	2 inlet per cylinder in Vee, 2 exhaust per cylinder laterally
Carburation	Lucas port fuel injection
Ignition	Lucas OPUS system
Sparking plugs	1 centrally placed 10mm plug per cylinder
Camshafts per bank	2 overhead
Gearbox	Hewland FG400
Brakes	Front outboard discs, rear inboard discs

Type	721X
Year of construction	1972
Number made	2
Frame designer	Robin Herd
Frame	as Type 721
Front suspension	as Type 721
Rear suspension	Triangulated wishbones, two forward running radius arms with inboard coil spring/damper units
Engine details	as Type 721
Gearbox	Alfa-Romeo 33/3 (later Hewland FG400)
Brakes	as Type 721
Type	721G
Year of construction	1972
Number made	5
Frame designer	Robin Herd
Frame	as Type 721 but smaller overall (as Type 722)
Front suspension	Double wishbones with outboard coil spring/damper units
Rear suspension	Lower wishbone, upper transverse link, two forward running radius arms with outboard coil spring/damper units
Engine details	as Type 721
Gearbox	Hewland FGA400
Brakes	Front outboard discs, rear outboard discs

Note: Frame modified in 1973 to include deformable structure in cockpit area

March 721/2 Surrounded at its press release by Niki Lauda, Max Mosley, Robin Herd and Phil Kerr, the 721 lost its 'Disco Volante' nose by its second race

The firm of March was founded in 1969 with Max Mosley, Alan Rees, Graham Coaker and Robin Herd as the leading lights— hence the name which is an anagram of their initials plus an 'A' for comfort. Max Mosley and Alan Rees had been involved in Formula 2 for some time and saw the need for a firm selling racing cars on a commercial basis, with prompt deliveries, after-sales service and good performance. Their first Formula 3 car appeared in 1969 and was quickly followed by Formula 1 and 2 cars for the 1970 season. These were described in contemporary reports as disappointing but, considering they were a first effort from a brand new team, perhaps too much was expected of them. The real disappointment was the 1971 Formula 1 car, the Type 711 (the first two figures denote the year and the third the class of racing). With a driver of the calibre of Ronnie Peterson, it really looked the part when it first appeared with its 'Disco Volante' front wing, but it never made the grade. Its best result was a second place in Monaco with Peterson driving. On the other hand their Formula 2 results were much more encouraging and March are still the dominant manufacturers in that Formula.

However, as regards Formula 1, many people thought 1972 would be a make-or-break year. The outcome was curious for there cannot be many instances where a constructor has brought out no fewer than three different models in one year, let alone five months!

721/1   As always March were prompt with their new models: the Type 721 was announced in December 1971 and three examples were ready to race at Buenos Aires in January 1972. The 721 proved to be an adapted version of the 711 and, at first, even had the same type of futuristic bodywork. The chassis construction and suspension was completely conventional, with the side-mounted radiators which made the strange frontal shape possible. The mandatory British standard Hewland FG400 gearbox and Cosworth DFV engine were fitted inside. March's golden boy, Ronnie Peterson, was to handle 721/1. A Swede, Peterson had come up the ladder at a great rate of knots, via Formula 3 and Formula 2. Almost from the start it was obvious that he was destined for great things and March were very lucky to sign him.

Surprisingly Peterson was far back on the grid for the Argentine GP, but this was because of illness. He did better in the race and,

despite a spin, gained the first World Championship points for the car with a good sixth place. From the outside this must have seemed a good result, but to those on the scene it was apparent that the new car was way off the pace. Immediately Robin Herd sat down with his pen and ink, although the results of his labours were not to be seen for several months.

In South Africa the factory cars reverted to the standard chisel nose and flaps used by most other side-radiator cars at this time. Peterson climbed as high as third, but a loose rear wing caused him to fall back and finish fifth.

The first ever Brazil GP was organised in 1972, a non-Championship race as a tryout for a World Championship race in 1973. March sent Peterson across with 721/1; in spite of being without a clutch and suffering a slowly deflating front tyre, he survived to finish a good second.

By this time the 721X was all the rage and 721/1 was taken to Spain and Monaco merely in case of accidents. The car only appeared once more—when Niki Lauda took it down to Vallelunga for the Gran Premio di Republica Italiana. He disgraced himself by crashing the car in practice and it had to be written off.

721/2   The car driven at first by Lauda had an even shorter career, appearing in just two races before disappearing into a limbo. Lauda was an Austrian who had bought his way on a rent-a-car basis into the March Formula 2 team in 1971. He had previous experience with Formula 3 cars and matured very quickly into a fine and sensible driver. It was plain to see that he, like Peterson, was one of the stars of the 1970s. The Argentine GP was only Lauda's second race; wisely he did not attempt any heroics, and started from the rear of the grid. Again in the race, Lauda took things gently but finished eleventh.

The car's second and final appearance was in the South African GP. Lauda was not on the back row this time and only lost one lap to the leader in the race, finishing an excellent seventh.

And that was that; the car was never to be seen again in Formula 1, although it is worth noting that Pescarolo crashed 721/3 on several occasions during the year and it may be that 721/2 became one of the replacement chassis.

721/3   Frank Williams had been in motor racing for many years.

A driver in the old Formula 3 circus days, and the originator of many apocryphal tales of derring-do in halls of ill repute throughout Europe, he graduated to wheeling and dealing. There is no doubt, however, that through all the smooth-talk image Williams is a completely dedicated man. His dearest—in fact, his only—ambition is to achieve the Championship of the World in one of his own cars. The saddest moment in his career came when his dear friend Piers Courage was killed in the de Tomaso in 1970. He took a long time to get over that. In 1971 he bought his first Formula 1 March for Henri Pescarolo to drive. He kept this car in 1972 for Carlos Pace, while buying 721/3 for Pescarolo. It was in 1972 that Pescarolo really entered into his own as a 'demolition agent' as he left a trail of destruction through Europe.

Things started fairly quietly with an eighth place in Argentina and an eleventh in South Africa. In Brazil the car stopped dead at the first corner, its throttle slides jammed by sand.

Back in England, Pescarolo had a really good drive in the International Trophy and was in the first six when a flying stone dislodged the airbox, which crushed a water pipe causing the engine to overheat.

After a slow eleventh, and last, place in Spain, Pescarolo journeyed to Monaco where in appalling weather he aquaplaned off a straight and smashed a couple of wheels.

The car was repaired for the Belgian GP and, although Pescarolo finished, he was miles behind after changing two tyres and having a sticking throttle replaced. In practice for the French GP, he had his second accident, when blinded by dust from another car; this time 721/3 was very badly damaged.

It was not ready for the British GP but it did not matter as Pescarolo crashed the new Williams. For the German GP he was back in the March which had a brand new monocoque constructed by Williams—and a fat lot of good it did, for Pescarolo had another enormous accident when in sixth place, almost destroying the poor car once more.

Williams again reconstructed it, using another new monocoque—only to have it destroyed in practice for the Austrian GP by the durable Frenchman. Apparently a tyre burst this time. If it wasn't so tragic for Williams, it would have been pure knockabout comedy.

In the Italian GP the team barely got as far as practice before Pescarolo crashed the car in unofficial practice. When the car came out on the Friday it had the old unicorn nose with Disco Volante front wing; this made one wonder whether this time Williams had taken the easy way out and 'obtained' from the works 721/2 which had disappeared earlier on. After the bump the car never handled well and Pescarolo failed to qualify for the race.

Across in America Pescarolo finished a race! His rear suspension had to be tightened up in the middle of the Canadian GP, but he made it, albeit in thirteenth and last place. He finished again in the United States GP—this time in fourteenth place.

Back in England for the final thrash of the year Pescarolo had a fitting end to the season when he spun and was hit by another competitor. Only the steering was damaged, but it was no surprise when Henri was given the 'here's your hat, what's the hurry' routine by Williams. The poor car lay down and died, and Frank Williams started on the construction of his own cars for the next season.

721/4 When the entry list for the 1972 South African GP was printed, it was not surprising to see Rolf Stommelen entered in an Eifelland, a car named after his long-time sponsors, Eifelland Wöhnwagenbau, the caravan firm. What a surprise it was though when the Eifelland Type 21 turned out to be none other than a March Type 721 wearing gents' natty suiting. It had the normal March unicorn nose, but the central bodywork had been redesigned by one Luigi Colani, its most bizarre feature being a central periscope-type rear-view mirror. Colani had also fitted it with 'the world's first progressive titanium springs'. But it was no faster than the conventional cars and through the season it gradually reverted to normal March practice. By the time Watson raced the car on behalf of Hexagon at the season's end it was a normal March in appearance. He gained a good sixth place, having been as high as third before the weather changed.

Stommelen's form in the car had been variable, but usually slow. He crashed in Spain and retired from the German GP with electrical trouble, but otherwise finished all his races. His final race with the car was in the Austrian GP; he had two pit stops when loose bodywork was secured, but finished in fifteenth spot.

Sadly for Stommelen, Eifelland Wöhnwagenbau were taken over and all support was withdrawn from both the Formula 1 entry and the extensive Formula 2 commitment. Stommelen was forced to sell the car to Hexagon and make a temporary retirement from racing. The car ended its days in Ireland.

721X/1 When Robin Herd designed the 721X he was trying to get a very low polar moment of inertia, which should increase the cornering power in the hands of a skilled driver like Peterson. On the other hand the breakaway point would be much more sudden. To this end Herd used an Alfa-Romeo gearbox internals placed in front of the crown wheel and pinion. The rear suspension was also different, consisting of triangulated wishbones working inboard coil spring/dampers. Apart from the monocoque being somewhat squarer, the chassis was otherwise much as before. In the Race of Champions Peterson, who had to stop to have a loose wheel fixed, finished eleventh. When the cars arrived in Spain it was clear that March had a disaster to cope with as they were just plain slow. Lauda, in 721X/1, retired after only seven laps with a sticking throttle. After another dismal performance in Monaco, it was obvious the cars were far too difficult to handle; although Lauda drove the car once more, he could only manage to finish twelfth.

The problem was, of course, the tremendous initial understeer followed by a very quick breakaway of the rear end. The memories work right back to the old Auto-Unions. In their original form, with the driver seated at the very front, only one man ever handled the cars to their absolute limit and that was the great Bernd Rosemeyer, surely one of the finest drivers of all. Lauda was good, but at that stage of his career not that good.

721X/2 The second car—which differed from the first in having certain parts made of titanium—was somewhat faster. Peterson drove it in the 1972 Spanish GP, but retired with mechanical problems, including trouble with the differential.

The Weismann differential was replaced on this car for the Monaco GP by a ZF unit. In spite of his usual frightening performance Peterson was well down the grid and had an eventful race, going straight on at the chicane, his steering wheel having come unscrewed, but was still eleventh.

Peterson appeared at the Oulton Park Gold Cup Race with the Alfa-Romeo gearbox replaced by a conventional Hewland FG400 to try to make the handling better, but little was proved as he ran into Wisell at the start and broke a wheel. At the Belgian GP

the car was fitted with a conventionally mounted gearbox and also the standard March 721 suspension, but it was no better and Peterson only managed to finish ninth. The cars were then discarded as the 721Gs were now ready.

721G/1 A great deal of interest was created at the Spanish GP by the arrival of Mike Beuttler's little team. Sponsored by a group of London stockbrokers, the team saw the answer to the problem of how to do a season of Formula 1 at reasonable cost—this was: to persuade a DFV engine to mate with a basic March Formula 2 chassis. This proved not difficult to do and with extra tankage an acceptable car was achieved. The chassis was much smaller than the Formula 1 chassis and handled much better as well.

The car was far from raceworthy in Spain and failed to qualify, but in Monaco Beuttler gained a thirteenth place. Being a private entrant he could not take the same liberties with his car as a factory driver could, it being essential that the car finished the year in one piece. In Belgium, Beuttler had a recurrence of an old March problem—breaking a drive shaft. It was notable that by now the factory drivers were looking at the 721G with ill-disguised interest and at Vallelunga Lauda tried out Beuttler's car. Beuttler had a good race here, finishing a creditable fourth.

The car was now thoroughly sorted out and Beuttler had a long string of fair results. He failed to finish the French GP when he ran out of fuel and the Austrian GP when the fuel metering unit failed, but other than that he went right through to the Brazil GP 1973 before his next retirement. It was a close thing in Canada, though, as he nearly knocked a wheel off and had to have a drive shaft and bottom link replaced at the pits.

After the South African GP in 1973, where Beuttler finished fifteenth following another crash necessitating the replacement of the front wheels, he returned the car to the factory who replaced it with an updated 721G/2. His old car thereupon received the same treatment and reappeared at Monaco on loan to Lec Refrigeration for David Purley to drive. It was barely recognisable from its last appearance, as the type of fuel tankage had been converted to conform with the new regulations, while the deformable structures had been attached and the rear track

March 721/4 and 721X/2 *Still early in their careers both cars had already been extensively modified—a bad sign indeed!*

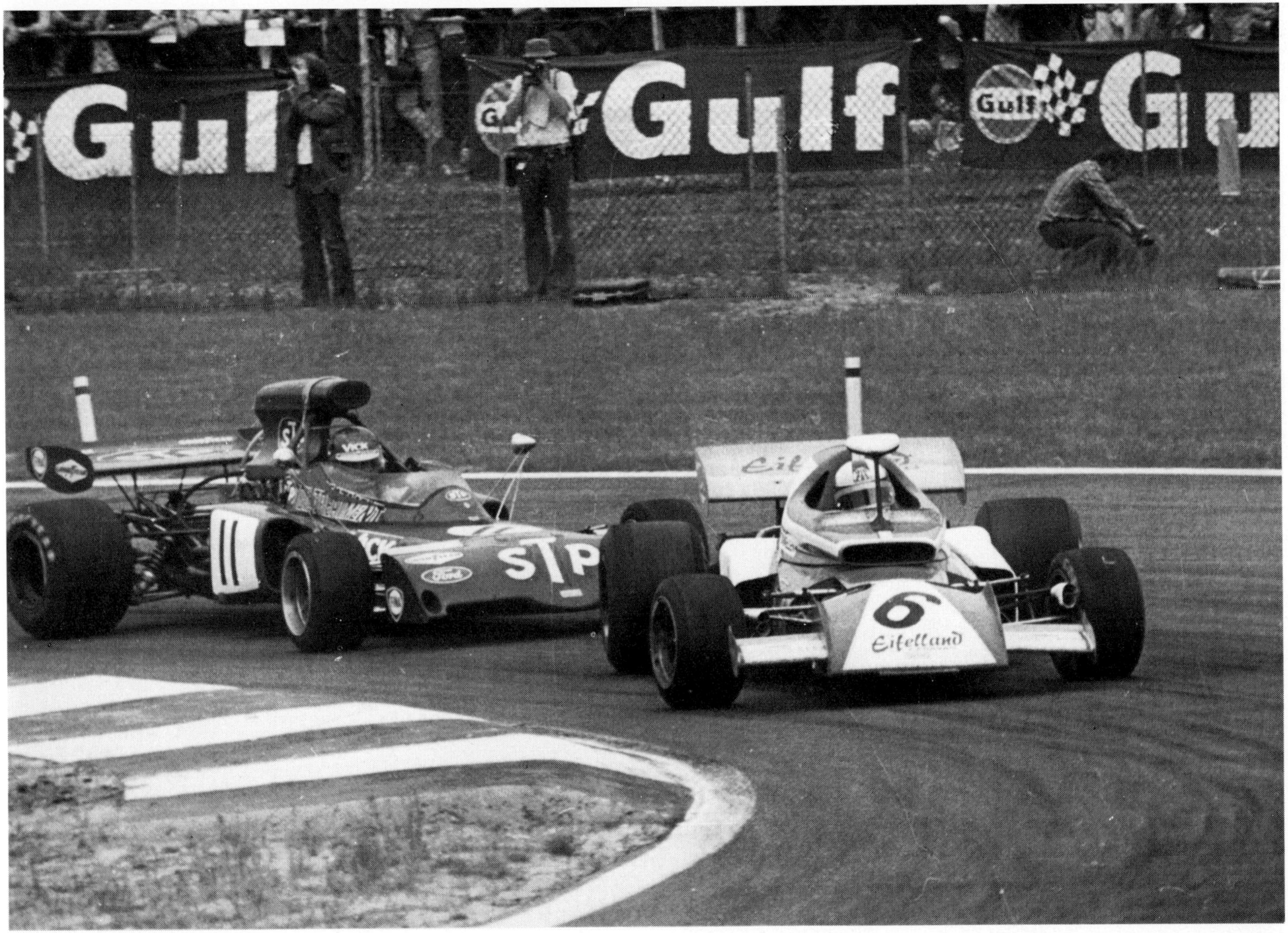

Gulf
Gulf
Gulf
Gulf
STP
Ford
Eifelland

narrowed. It was generally referred to as a 731, but how a car can change its type in mid-flight I do not know. It is like a Lotus 72 suddenly becoming a 72D when the chassis is the same; it cannot be done, so in this book 721Gs they will remain.

Purley drove well in his first race until a fuel leak intervened. For the Swedish race, Reine Wisell was loaned the car but, after being the fastest March driver in practice, failed to make the start when a suspension bolt broke.

The car was returned to David Purley for the next few races. At Silverstone he disgraced himself by crashing the car in practice and not even making the start. In Zandvoort he stopped at the scene of Williamson's dreadful accident and tried in vain to rescue the hapless driver. Naturally after such an experience Purley could not carry on racing and retired to the pits.

Following a steady fifteenth place in Germany, the works repossessed the car for Jarier to drive. This action seemed justified when he got up to sixth place in the Austrian GP, before an old problem of fuel feed trouble recurred. Purley had another go at Monza, finishing a good ninth after a spin at the chicane.

The car's final two appearances were both in the hands of Jarier in America. He crashed towards the end of each race, but was classified eleventh in the United States.

721G/2 Following the admiration accorded to Beuttler's car, the factory admitted failure with the 721X and buckled down to the task of building three cars for their own drivers. These appeared in remarkable time; 721G/2 was then referred to as a development car and in due course Lauda was to have 721G/4. In France, Lauda did not get very far, breaking another driveshaft. After this 721G/2 became the factory spare car and never raced again in this form.

At the beginning of 1973, 721G/2 was modified like the other cars to 731 specifications and hired out or sold to Mike Beuttler for his year's activities. The result was an immediate improvement, for in his old car Beuttler had gradually been falling back down the field, but in the new one he had a good seventh in the 1973 Spanish GP. There was a lot of 'aggro' at the Belgian GP concerning the state of the track which broke up during the race. Beuttler was one of those to fall foul of it, but suffered no lasting injury to himself or the car.

Reine Wisell borrowed Beuttler's car for the French GP as Mike had been injured in a Formula 2 accident. Wisell had a most uncomfortable race as a fuel leak dripped fuel on to his seat. Luckily the car overheated and he had to retire anyway.

After this, Beuttler—not as reliable as the previous year—continued on his merry way. He had two minor bumps: in Germany, where he kept going; and in Austria, when rammed from behind by Hailwood, where he did not.

Beuttler's star performance in the latter half of the season was in the Italian GP. He was eighth at the start of the race, but a puncture and gear-linkage failure caused his retirement. His final drive in the car was in the United States GP, when he achieved a tenth place.

721G/3 Peterson's car was also ready at the French GP and he was immediately far happier than he had been in the 721X. This was destined to be the most famous of all the Marches. Peterson started it off on the right course with a fine fifth place, having been as high as third before a roll bar broke. He had another good drive at Brands Hatch, where he was fourth when he ran out of fuel on a corner and spun off into two already parked cars. He spun again in Germany, but lost little time and came back to gain his best place of the year in third.

He nearly had to retire in Austria when the fuel pressure started to sag, but after a pit stop twelfth place was achieved. Italy was a sad story as well: after a troublesome practice, Peterson just could not get the car to go and finished ninth.

So it was across to America where Peterson had a superb race until he crashed while attempting to pass Graham Hill. He had led for the first few laps and then been second until the unfortunate bump. The United States GP provided another demonstration of Peterson's prowess. He had broken two engines in practice, but came charging through the field to achieve a splendid fourth place.

But for the weather Peterson might have won the World Championship Victory Race; he led the first (wet) thirteen laps until the track dried and he had to stop to have the tyres changed, so that he dropped to eighth place at the end.

Peterson and Lauda now left the team as March could not

March 721X/1 Seen at its press release, the unconventional 721X was to be a bitter disappointment to its designer, Robin Herd

afford to run a factory team in the same way that Lotus could. In 1973 March ran just one car and even that was hired out if the money was right.

So it was that 721G/3 was converted to 731 specifications and appeared at Monaco. It marked the spectacular entry to Grand Prix racing of the extrovert Lord Hesketh, complete with huge yacht—or perhaps small liner. Pretty well off, Hesketh did not need a sponsor and could enjoy himself to his heart's content 'playing at Grand Prix racing'. Anyone who does this should, by tradition, toddle around at the wrong end of the race, acting as a mobile chicane. If Hesketh wished to play at it, he made a cardinal error in hiring as his driver the estimable James Hunt—formerly known as Shunt, he had outgrown the cognomen and showed great promise. Hesketh also hired a demon mechanical director with the unbelievable name of Harvey Postlethwaite. In his first race Hunt did reasonably well until near the end when his engine broke.

The team decided to miss the Swedish GP so that they could completely sort out the new car. At last things began to happen for March, and Hunt earned his first Championship point by taking a well-earned sixth place.

Hunt avoided the famous pile-up in the British GP and even profited from it in that he had a blank space in front of him on the re-start grid. He made the most of this and was up in third place for the major part of the race, until a blister appeared in a front tyre which dropped him to fourth. A large factor in this race was surely a brand new airbox from the demon Postlethwaite pen; at this time Hesketh led the way in the kinkiest airbox league. After the terrible accident to Roger Williamson in the Dutch GP, Hunt's third place went largely unnoticed.

Following this, the team gave the Nurburgring a miss in order to get down to some development work. This resulted in a new nose cone, named by the team 'Silly Nose' (it was that sort of team). The car also showed a redesigned wing and slightly different suspension work. All this was of no use in the Austrian GP when the fuel metering unit failed.

Hunt made a boo-boo in practice for the Italian GP and, rather than put the American trip at risk, the team returned to England to repair the car. By now everyone was expecting Hunt to go well and, if anything, his sixth place in Canada was a disappointment; so it was very exciting at Watkins Glen when he put the car on to the second row of the grid. The race was no anti-climax

and Hunt failed by only .312 seconds to beat Peterson, having chased him from flag to flag—a splendid end to the season indeed.

Hunt had not entirely finished with the car and had several drives with it in 1974 until the new Hesketh was finished. Hunt again staggered the racing world at the Argentine GP by taking the lead on the first lap, but the crafty Peterson psyched him into a spin at the next corner, the radiator intake clogged up, the engine overheated and that was that.

The car was gradually falling behind, however; at Interlagos a ninth place was all that could be managed, and it retired in the Brasilia non-Championship race. By now the new car was ready and everyone thought that was the end—Formula 5000 and the Donington Collection. But no, the 721G/3 made a final but rather pathetic appearance. It had been bought by Dempster International Racing Team for their ex Formula 3 protégé, Mike Wilds, to drive in the British GP, but it did not handle too well and he was unable to qualify this famous machine.

721G/4 Lauda's proper car was ready for the British GP and he was making progress with it. At least he was now competitive with the also-rans, but at this stage who could have seen him becoming Ferrari No 1 driver in under two years. Lauda gained a ninth place in the race and for the rest of the season ran around in midfield positions. In Germany he retired early on with a leaking oil tank, and at Monza was thwarted by Peterson, who put some wheels on the dirt which sprayed up over Lauda just behind and jammed his throttle slides. Similar jamming occurred in Canada, where it resulted in disqualification when outside assistance was needed to restart.

Lauda's final race with the machine was in the United States GP, where the fuel injection system played up and he failed to be classified.

In 1973 the car was immediately taken over by Jarier who was to be the official driver for the year. In Formula 2, Jarier was stunning, but he failed to show in Formula 1 until 1975. He started off on a bad note with the gearbox playing up at the first three races.

At Barcelona Jarier was not available to drive the car, which

March 721G/1 Saviour of the works team, Mike Beuttler races the original 721G in the 1972 British GP

had been brought up to 731 specifications; his seat went to Pescarolo who got an eighth place when everyone else retired.

Jarier was back for the next race but his luck failed to change: a crash, gearbox trouble, throttle linkage and constant velocity joint—it all happened to Jarier.

So, when Tom Wheatcroft offered some loot to the factory for a car for his protégé, Roger Williamson, to drive in the British GP, the car was quickly handed over. Williamson was a tremendously promising driver. The previous years he had walked over the opposition in the Wheatcroft March Formula 3 car and had made spectacular progress in Formula 2. He was truly a driver in the Peterson/Lauda mould, obviously destined for the top. Sadly his career was to be tragically cut short for, after being involved in the Scheckter incident at the British GP, Williamson was entered for the Dutch race. Early on he crashed at high speed. The car overturned and slowly caught fire. David Purley, who stopped his car and valiantly tried to release Williamson, was eventually driven back by the flames. By the time the fire was extinguished by the tardy marshals, Williamson was dead.

721G/5 Right at the end of the 1972 season—at the very last race, in fact—enthusiasts were surprised to see a brand new 721G in the paddock. It was destined for one Daniel Rouveyran to use in hill climbs, but unfortunately never made it as the driver for the day, François Migault, wrote it off on the second lap of practice.

March, despite their loud noises, have probably always been underfinanced for their Formula 1 efforts, certainly from 1973 onwards, but that does not explain their failure in 1972 when they managed three different models. It was a brave effort, all the same. That it failed in 1972 was probably because March tried to do too much at once with the interim Type 721 and the blind alley of the 721X before settling on the best of the three, the 721G. By 1973, when the car was properly sorted out by Harvey Postlethwaite, it was a little bit too late. The great drivers had gone and, quite understandably, Hunt did not have the experience to make the best use of the car when it was most competitive. But, by gum, he certainly tried, and who is to say that Peterson would have done any better?

Results

Year and race	Chassis number and result					
1972	721/1	721/2	721/3	721/4	721X/1	721X/2
Argentine GP	Peterson 6	Lauda 11	Pescarolo 8			
South African GP	Peterson 5	Lauda 7	Pescarolo 11	Stommelen 13		
Race of Champions				Stommelen 10	Peterson 11	
Brazil GP	Peterson 2		Pescarolo R			
International Trophy			Pescarolo R			
Spanish GP	Peterson S		Pescarolo 11	Stommelen C	Lauda R	Peterson R
					Peterson P	
Monaco GP	Peterson P		Pescarolo C	Stommelen 10	Lauda 16	Peterson 11
Gold Cup Race						Peterson C
Belgian GP			Pescarolo 16	Stommelen 11	Lauda 12	Peterson 9
GP Repub. Italiana	Lauda P/C		Pescarolo R			
French GP			Pescarolo P/C	Stommelen 16		
British GP				Stommelen 10		
German GP			Pescarolo C	Stommelen R		
Austrian GP			Pescarolo P/C	Stommelen 15		
Italian GP			Pescarolo NQ			
Canadian GP			Pescarolo 13			
United States GP			Pescarolo 14			
World Championship VR			Pescarolo R	Watson 6		

Results

Year and race	Chassis number and result				
1972	721G/1	721G/2	721G/3	721G/4	721G/5
Spanish GP	Beuttler NQ				
Monaco GP	Beuttler 13				
Belgian GP	Beuttler R				
GP Repub. Italiana	Beuttler 4				
	Lauda P				
French GP	Beuttler R	Lauda R	Peterson 5		
British GP	Beuttler 13		Peterson 7	Lauda 9	
German GP	Beuttler 8		Peterson 3	Lauda R	
Austrian GP	Beuttler R	Peterson P	Peterson 12	Lauda 10	
Italian GP	Beuttler 10	Peterson S	Peterson 9	Lauda 13	
Canadian GP	Beuttler 15		Peterson D	Lauda D	
United States GP	Beuttler 13		Peterson 4	Lauda 19	
World Championship VR	Beuttler 11		Peterson 8		Migault P/C
1973					
Argentine GP	Beuttler 10			Jarier R	
Brazil GP	Beuttler R			Jarier R	
South African GP	Beuttler 15			Jarier 13	
Spanish GP		Beuttler 7		Pescarolo 8	
Belgian GP		Beuttler 11		Jarier 12	
Monaco GP	Purley R	Beuttler R	Hunt R/9	Jarier R	
Swedish GP	Wisell P	Beuttler 8		Jarier R	
French GP		Wisell R	Hunt 6	Jarier R	

Results

Year and race	Chassis number and result				
1973	721G/1	721G/2	721G/3	721G/4	721G/5
British GP	Purley P/C	Beuttler 11	Hunt 4	Williamson C	
Dutch GP	Purley R	Beuttler R	Hunt 3	Williamson C	
German GP	Purley 15	Beuttler 16			
Austrian GP	Jarier R	Beuttler C	Hunt R		
Italian GP	Purley 9	Beuttler R	Hunt P/C		
Canadian GP	Jarier 19	Beuttler R	Hunt 7		
United States GP	Jarier 11/C	Beuttler 10	Hunt 2		
1974					
Argentine GP			Hunt R		
Brazil GP			Hunt 9		
GP Pres. Medici			Hunt R		
British GP			Wilds NQ		

C=Crash ; D=disqualified ; NQ=non-qualifier ; P=practice car only ; R=retired ; S=spare car not used

Matra

MS11 and MS120

Type	MS11
Year of construction	1968
Number made	3
Frame designer	Bernard Boyer
Frame	Full-length riveted and glued aluminium monocoque chassis with front suspension on a bulkhead and rear suspension on a cross member
Front suspension	Lower wishbone, upper rocker arm operating inboard coil spring/damper units
Rear suspension	Lower wishbone, upper transverse link, two forward running radius arms with outboard coil spring/damper units
Engine make	Matra
Engine designer	Georges Martin
Engine type	MS12
Engine capacity	2993cc
Cylinders	12 in 60° Vee formation
Bore and stroke	79.7mm x 50.0mm
Valves per cylinder	2 inlet per cylinder between camshafts, 2 exhaust per cylinder laterally
Carburation	Lucas port fuel injection
Ignition	Lucas OPUS system
Sparking plugs	1 centrally placed 10mm plug per cylinder
Camshafts per bank	2 overhead
Gearbox	Hewland FG400 (Hewland DG300 used in one car at first two races)
Brakes	Outboard discs

Matra MS11/02   At the 1968 British GP where the car was driven by Beltoise, its Formula 2 parentage can clearly be seen

Type	MS120
Year of construction	1970-2
Number made	7
Frame designer	Bernard Boyer
Frame	Riveted aluminium 2 box section monocoque containing rubber fuel cells. Rear part of chassis formed by crankcase of engine bolted to centre section. Front suspension on a bulkhead, rear suspension on cross member.
Front suspension	Lower wishbone, upper transverse link located by forward and backward running short radius arms. Outboard coil spring/damper unit.
Rear suspension	Lower wishbone, upper transverse link, two forward running radius arms with outboard coil spring/damper units.
Engine make	Matra
Engine designer	Georges Martin
Engine type	MS12 and MS71
Engine capacity	2993cc
Cylinders	12 in 60° Vee formation
Bore and stroke	79.7mm x 50.0mm
Valves per cylinder	2 inlet per cylinder between camshafts, 2 exhausts per cylinder laterally
Carburation	Lucas port fuel injection
Ignition	Lucas OPUS system
Sparking plugs	1 centrally placed 10mm plug per cylinder
Camshafts per bank	2 overhead
Gearbox	Hewland FG400
Brakes	Front outboard discs, rear inboard discs

Matra MS120/01   When it reappeared in 1970 the Formula 1 Matra had changed drastically. Here is Beltoise in the Spanish GP of that year

Matra entered motor racing in the mid-1960s via Formula 3 and then Formula 2, having previously been involved in the French aircraft industry. They had become very successful in the smaller classes. Jean-Pierre Beltoise gained Matra's first big win in the Rheims Formula 3 race in 1965. They went on to enter two teams in Formula 2 races: one was the official factory team under the Matra Sports banner; the other, run from Britain by Ken Tyrrell, called itself Matra International. This was the situation at the end of 1967 when Matra and Tyrrell resolved to enter Formula 1 racing. Tyrrell decided to use the British Cosworth engine, and his chassis was ready first for Stewart to drive. Matra Sports also used a Cosworth engine in an MS10 chassis, until the MS11 chassis and the V12 engine, known as the MS12, was ready at the 1968 Monaco GP.

MS11 01 As is often the case, the prototype of a new design tends to be a bit of a hack and this car was no exception. It followed the design of the MS10 with a riveted and glued aluminium monocoque of full length to support the engine. The front suspension was hung on a bulkhead and the rear suspension on a cross member. Front suspension was by wishbone and rocker arm with inboard coilspring/dampers but outboard brakes, while the rear suspension was standard with transverse link, wishbone, and radius arms with outboard coil spring/dampers and brakes.

The engine was a normal 60° V12 with four valves per cylinder and single plugs. The exhaust ports were lateral, ending in six tail pipes. The inlet ports and plugs were inserted between the two camshafts. All very fine and it sounded beautiful, but it did not develop any power, or at least not as much as the opposition did. For the Monaco GP, 01 was fitted with the new light FG400 gearbox, but the car was only used in practice by Beltoise. It raced for the first time at Spa when Beltoise finished a poor seventh. The car was underpowered and he had trouble with the gear change as well as having to stop for fuel.

As the car was low on power it was lucky that the next race—the Dutch GP—was so wet. The car had a DG300 gearbox refitted as the FG400 had been transferred to 02. The engine was fitted with a new exhaust system which improved matters a little, but the car still had problems. In common with most other drivers, Beltoise spun twice in the race and called at the pits to

have the throttle slides flushed with petrol; after that he went really well and tigered his way back up the field to finish second.

Beltoise only took the newer of his cars to the French and British GPs, but 01 appeared at the Nurburgring as a practice car, now fitted with its own FG400 gearbox—both cars thus had the newer, lighter gearbox. 01's next race was not until the American series when it became his regular car, but proved no more successful than 02. After changing the battery twice, Beltoise was forced to retire when the gearbox stripped in Canada. A drive shaft fractured in the United States and 01's career finished when a left rear wishbone pulled away from its mounting.

MS11 02 Appearing at Monaco with 01, 02 was the lighter of the two cars and the one Beltoise elected to race; but he was forced to retire when he hit a kerb and bent the front suspension rocker arm. For the Dutch GP the FG400 gearbox was transferred from 01 and was retained all season, but Beltoise raced 01 at Zandvoort and kept 02 in reserve. The car did not even go to Spa as it was being prepared at the factory for the French GP. Jo Schlesser lost his life in that race and Beltoise was badly affected by the accident. Although he carried on, it was without enthusiasm and he finished ninth.

And so the 1968 season continued its depressing record, with an engine failure in Britain and a crash at the Nurburgring. The car was then fitted with yet another new exhaust system. At Monza Beltoise finally reached the finishing line and gained some points for fifth place. This was the last appearance of 02 for it was not taken to America.

MS11 03 When Henri Pescarolo, the bearded Frenchman, joined the team a new car was provided for him. It was still fitted with the old exhaust pipes at his first appearance, which was in the Canadian GP. Pescarolo never showed high up the field and retired with low oil pressure. He was unable to get an entry for the United States GP although he did practise, but in 01. His second and last race was in Mexico where he finished an unstable ninth.

So it was that after a very brief spell Matra Sports withdrew from racing. There were several reasons for this. The engine was not developing nearly enough power to compete on even terms in Formula 1 at this time. The firm had decided to put its major effort in 1969 into a real crack at winning the Le Mans twenty-four-hour race. Finally the Tyrrell team had been reasonably successful for a first season's effort and Matra wanted to back them as far as they could, especially as Tyrrell had one of the top drivers in the world in Jackie Stewart.

The plan had partly paid off when Stewart gained the World Championship in 1969, although Le Mans was not won. In view of the financial situation, however, it became imperative for the firm to sell its sports cars in some numbers and the decision was taken to merge the operations of the Chrysler/Simca company and Matra. As a result of this, it was thought that as a marketing policy Matra ought to be in Formula 1 racing on their own account and with their own engines, not using the rival Ford. So Matra re-entered the field of Formula 1 in 1970. They used the same two drivers, Beltoise and Pescarolo, and again three cars were built for the season, all virtually identical.

MS120 01 As in the MS11 series the first car was a hack, but it really impressed on its first excursion at Kyalami in the South African GP, not least for its noise which recalled some of the great sounding cars of the past. Its construction followed that of competitors rather than the MS11 in that the riveted aluminium two-box section monocoque ended at the rear of the cockpit, with the back half of the chassis being formed by the engine. The rear suspension was standard, while the front suspension differed somewhat in having a lower wishbone supporting the coil spring/damper unit but above a single transverse link located by two short radius arms running forward and backwards from it. The engine was similar to the previous one except that the inlet ports were now placed in the Vee.

After a good fourth place in the South African GP the car faded into the background at the next outing, the Race of Champions. The handling had always been twitchy compared with the front runners, and eventually Beltoise had his accident in practice when he not only ripped off two wheels but also crinkled the fragile monocoque chassis. This was quickly repaired and the car became the factory spare and mobile supply of parts. It was crashed again by Pescarolo in the British GP and, after being taken to America as a spare car for Beltoise

in the three Grand Prix, it faded from the scene and was never used competitively again.

MS120 02 The car used throughout 1970 by the taciturn Henri Pescarolo was the second in the series, but he was never really fast enough to be in the front line of Grand Prix drivers. Add to this the fact that the engine was 15 BHP down on the Cosworth DFV and the outcome was an unsatisfactory season. It is strange that all the way through the present Formula the pundits have said the V12 engine is going to be *the* engine to go for. So many have tried, but still the old Cosworth engine goes on and on winning races. It all boils down to weight. Because the V12 engine is heavier, it must give considerably more power than the Cosworth engine to overcome not only the weight of the engine but the increased weight of fuel that must also be carried. It took until 1975 for a 12 cylinder car to conquer the simplicity of the V8.

In 02's first race the handling was far from good and the car was seventh. But it was the engine that caused most problems: a con rod broke when Pescarolo was in third place in the 1970 Spanish GP, an engine blew up in practice at Spa and another in practice for the Dutch GP. Considering an engine change took about seven or eight hours, it must have been a galling experience for the mechanics. A fraught time was had at Auvergne where, following oil pressure trouble, the car was crashed and then suffered a shock-absorber malfunction, making it a surprise to finish in fifth place. The chassis was later found to have been twisted in the crash and, after a straightening operation, it must have been nice to have a trouble-free run into sixth position in the German GP.

The engine problems were not over, as another change had to be made in practice for the Austrian GP and two more blow-ups occurred in a private practice session before the Italian GP. Here the car retired with a broken valve spring. The final act was another engine failure, this time a broken con rod, in practice for the Canadian GP.

After this the car mended its ways and Pescarolo finished the season with a run of mid-field placings, despite a gearbox problem in the Mexican GP which caused him to call at the pits.

The team was greatly strengthened in 1971 by the replacement of Pescarolo by Chris Amon, late of March but previously No 1 driver with Ferrari. Amon had acquired a reputation like Stirling Moss of being a jinx driver. He had come close to victory on several occasions, but the chequered flag always eluded him in Formula 1 until he had a win in a non-Championship race with the Type 701 March. In spite of this jinx, there can be no doubt that Amon was one of the top five in the late '60s and early '70s.

Invariably a new driver brings fresh heart to a struggling team and Amon paralysed the rest of the field in the non-Championship race in Argentina at the beginning of 1971. He easily scored what turned out to be the MS120's only Formula 1 victory. Like the March 721G, this was a finish on a high note for 02. It was taken to several more races as a spare, finally being pensioned off when 06 was completed in time for the Monaco GP.

MS120 03   As the car of the team leader, Jean-Pierre Beltoise, 03 was the one which the team concentrated on in 1970. In fact, it was already modified from the original specifications by the time it appeared in the 1970 Spanish GP. With 13in wheels, in place of the standard 15in type, new brake discs, aerofoil and titanium rear hubs, it was clear that an improvement in the road-holding department was sought after the South African GP. As well as these modifications, the car had the more powerful engine and an integral front upright caliper. Pescarolo's car in Spain had been similarly modified.

The engine seized in the Spanish GP, but the main problem turned out to be overheating at the front end. For Monaco, therefore, it was extra cooling for the front brake and back to the 15in wheels. The higher speeds at Spa meant easier cooling and, in the interests of smaller frontal area air flow respectively, the 13in wheels could be re-adopted and the front brake coolers abandoned.

Things were now progressing well and Beltoise had third and fifth places to show for it. For the slower circuits the 15in wheels were again adopted, but a recurring problem was that of understeer; so for the French GP different anti-roll bars and new camber angles were used. The effect was dramatic, for Beltoise was consistently fast in practice and led the race until a sad puncture followed by fuel starvation spoilt the joy.

For some reason, perhaps a short illness suffered by Beltoise, the team did not follow up their promising showing in France. Lots of engine trouble occurred, although Beltoise did get a sixth

place in Austria. At Monza, the team introduced a new T series engine with a stiffer crankcase and special con rods to permit higher revving, but this was not pursued even though Beltoise finished third for his best placing of the year. America was a disaster with more engine, tyre and suspension breakdowns. Beltoise nevertheless managed a fifth place in the Mexican GP, where the car had two ignition systems—the regular and an experimental one.

Matra Sports were producing a new car for the 1971 season, but it was not ready for the first races and Chris Amon had to make do with 03 for a while. It had been updated to a certain extent for the South African GP by a 1971 engine which had modified injection and exhaust systems. After a good practice session Amon suffered power loss in the race and could finish only fifth. For the non-Championship Questor GP the car used a 1970 engine as the firm did not wish to risk the new one in an unimportant race. Despite this handicap Amon improved a little by finishing fourth.

The car went out in a blaze of glory in the Spanish GP when Amon had a storming third place. Beltoise now had his new car, named the MS120B, and by the next race Amon would have his as well.

MS120B 04   When the new models appeared there were many detail changes, mainly in the shape of the monocoque which had differently shaped slab sides to allow more fuel to be carried for the thirsty V12 engine. Amon celebrated the arrival of his new car in the International Trophy with the fastest practice time. Although he had trouble in the first heat, this was cured and in the other heat a good second place was achieved. The problem was with fuel pump pressure and this recurred at Monaco, although the final straw, which caused the retirement, was crown wheel and pinion failure. This fault also affected 05.

The car had a new experience at Zandvoort where it was crashed in wet weather by Amon and missed the next two races. It was not raced again that season being taken along as a spare car to the German and Italian GPs.

This situation seemed to continue at first in 1972 but, at Monaco, Amon found it to be better than 06. After four pit stops to clear a misting vizor a sixth place was achieved, the other cars having had even more trouble than Amon did.

When the new car appeared it really seemed to be the end of the road for 04. But, at the British GP, Amon had an unfortunate incident in practice with 07 and the damage could not be repaired for the race. So he was forced to use 04, but lost a whole lap at the start after a slight bump with Mike Beuttler. He had a grand race up through the field, so that again a Matra finished in a blaze of glory in fourth place.

Although the car was taken to the next three races it was only as a spare. Its only use was quite an interesting one—Niki Lauda drove it in an unofficial practice session and blew the engine up.

MS120B 05

Jean-Pierre Beltoise had missed a few races before the 1971 Spanish GP, as a result of being suspended. In a sports car race in South America his car failed on the circuit and, in contravention of the rules, he pushed it along the track. While he was doing this, the Italian, Ignazio Giunti, ran into the car and was tragically killed. Beltoise' suspension was lifted for the Spanish race.

As the only Frenchman in the team, it was only right that he should have the first of the MS120Bs to appear. It had the new engine which had a modified exhaust system, different camshafts and a modified crankshaft. After an uneventful race Beltoise managed an uninspired sixth. Presumably he was still suffering reactions from the crash in South America. A couple of retirements followed, but the ninth place he gained in the Dutch GP was better than it seemed as he was the first runner on Goodyear tyres to finish.

The CSI of the FIA heaped coals of fire on Beltoise' head when they handed out a further period of suspension for the South American incident. Quite what they hoped to gain by this is debatable but, if he was at fault, Beltoise had certainly had sufficient punishment already. Neither he nor the car appeared again until the Canadian GP. Here, at last, the engine power problems had been sorted out by means of revised porting, and the monocoque had been strengthened behind the driver. These were the same modifications that had been carried out on 06 by the time the Italian GP was run. In the Canadian GP, Beltoise had the best start to a race all season and lay third until he crashed on the sixteenth lap.

His last appearance with the Matra Grand Prix team was in the United States GP where he finished eighth in spite of loss of power and poor front brakes. This also proved to be the final appearance of 05 as it was pensioned off at the end of the season.

MS120B 06

The last of the MS120B types appeared as Amon's spare car at the 1971 Monaco GP. Immediately afterwards, at the Dutch GP, the car had been fitted with the MS71 engine which had a completely new cylinder head. Again it was only used in practice, but when 04 was crashed Amon had to use 06 in the French GP. He finished fifth, in spite of consuming a number of valve springs in the new engine. The engine trouble persisted in the two following races and was so bad that Amon used an old engine in the German GP, but he only succeeded in crashing the car. For this race, as well as the old engine the whole rear end from 04 was grafted on to the rear of 06.

Seemingly endless trouble was caused at this time by the unique wheels that Matra Sports used. At normal racing pressures these caused air to leak from the tyres. As a temporary expedient they were run at a higher pressure in the Dutch GP. This unfortunately resulted in excessive understeer which could only be corrected by making new wheels.

It is clear that, at this stage, all was not well with the team. Development was static, if not retrogressive, and the political situation at base camp was such that decisions were taken too slowly, allowing the other teams to draw ahead. Eventually the only solution was to miss a Grand Prix in order to get the cars completely race-worthy.

When 06 re-appeared it had the modifications which were carried out a little later on 05, and showed immediate results when Amon was fastest in practice. It is always a bit risky to miss a race in order to become more competitive, because on occasions it has happened that a team has fallen even further behind. But this did not seem to have been the case here. In the race Amon was always among the front runners, leading on many occasions, but sadly he lost his vizor and dropped back to finish sixth.

In the American series it was not as successful. Canada was wet and Amon could only manage tenth. In the United States GP he had to stop to change a wheel and this dropped him to twelfth place at the end.

In early 1972 the car remained as the mainstay of the team and was used as a type of workshop for the new 07. It had completely new front suspension in the Argentine, but owing to an incorrectly assembled gearbox it was unable to start the race. Further modifications were carried out from race to race. In South Africa the oil tank had been moved to the rear of the car. By the Spanish GP, 35kg weight had been shed—long overdue, this reduction had been achieved in a variety of ways: titanium was used for the exhaust system, the rear wing enclosed a lighter honeycomb structure and new light alloy wheels were fitted. But in the race the gearbox overheated and the car never showed its potential.

It was used only in practice at Monaco before being cannibalised for 04's use. On its final appearance, in the 1972 Belgian GP, 06 consumed two engines in practice but nevertheless followed precedent by going out like a lion. Amon lay in a fine third place at one time, but had to stop for fuel and dropped to sixth place by the end.

MS120C 07 Amon was pleased to see a completely new car for him at the 1972 French GP. But, if the truth be known, it was not quite as new as it might appear. Admittedly it had a brand new, stiffer and bulbous— as opposed to slab-sided—monocoque, but all the mechanical components came from 06. This sort of situation would not have happened the previous year when Matra used to arrive with tons of spares. Now the whole set-up seemed to be run on a much tighter budget.

This did not affect Amon who was delighted with the car. Easily fastest in practice, he led the race till over half distance; it was desperately sad when a front tyre punctured and he dropped to ninth place. However, he came charging back through the field in a masterly fashion to finish a fine third in his best drive for Matra.

Yet again the impetus was not maintained—the car was crashed in practice for the British GP, ignition failure lost over a lap at the start of the German GP, and a broken cam lobe on the morning of the United States GP could not be changed. Amon therefore started from the back of the grid and stayed there. In the meantime the only good performance was at Monza where Amon was in the leading three, until a brake pad wore out and the brake then seized. In the Canadian GP the exhaust system broke but, for once, Amon kept going to finish in sixth place.

The United States GP in 1972 proved to be the final appearance of the MS120 Matra Formula 1 car. The cars returned to the factory and were never raced again. The engines, however, achieved great success, powering the Matra-Simca sports cars into domination of the class. As far as Formula 1 racing is concerned, though, frequent rumours continue to circulate. At first, it was said, Amon was going to use the engines in a car of his own design. Then various other teams, such as Shadow, tried to come to terms with Matra to use the engine in a proprietary chassis, but it has taken until 1976 for the engine to be regularly in Formula 1. The new firm, run by Guy Ligier, has fitted the engines into a car of his own construction.

It is difficult to see why Matra failed so dismally in Formula 1 racing, but probably the answer is multiple.

In the first place, they had it far too easy in Formula 3 and Formula 2, and indeed later with the Cosworth-engined Formula 1 car with which Stewart won the World Championship. They did not appreciate the advantage they had over the other teams in having Stewart to drive their cars.

In the second place, the engine only gave its full power potential on rare occasions, as is obvious from the results.

In the third place, the drivers Matra engaged were not of the highest calibre. In the beginning they tried to keep an all-French team. Pescarolo was not altogether reliable, while Beltoise was more handicapped by the arm injured many years previously than anyone would admit. Later they signed Amon who, although very quick, was all too easily put off by trifling faults instead of soldiering on as, say, Rodriguez would have done. For instance, Amon sacrificed a sure third place in the 1972 South African GP by stopping to complain about an obscure vibration for which no cause could be found.

In the fourth place, decisions on modifications took far too long to be arrived at. In other words, a Colin Chapman type was missing and this enabled Matra's competitors to get ahead at important times.

In the fifth place, and most important, there was a lack of impulsion which was reminiscent of Ferrari when they were trying to do too much at once. Matra had the same trouble at the time of their Formula 1 efforts when they were also making a big push for a Le Mans win and the World Sports Car Championship. It is in the sports car field that they have since had the tremendous worldwide success that their dedicated team undeniably deserves.

Nevertheless the world of Formula 1 racing would have been much the poorer if these spectacular cars had never appeared. If nothing else, they brought a new dimension to the noise level of Grand Prix motor racing.

Results

Year and race	Chassis number and result		
1968	MS11/01	MS11/02	MS11/03
Monaco GP	Beltoise P	Beltoise C	
Belgian GP	Beltoise 8	Beltoise P	
Dutch GP	Beltoise 2		
French GP		Beltoise 9	
British GP		Beltoise R	
		Stewart P	
German GP	Beltoise P	Beltoise C	
Italian GP		Beltoise 5	
Canadian GP	Beltoise R		Pescarolo R
United States GP	Beltoise R		Beltoise P
	Pescarolo P		
Mexican GP	Beltoise R		Pescarolo 9

Results

Year and race	Chassis number and result						
1970	MS120/01	MS120/02	MS120/03	MS120B/04	MS120B/05	MS120B/06	MS120C/07
South African GP	Beltoise 4	Pescarolo 7					
Race of Champions	Beltoise P/C						
Spanish GP		Pescarolo R	Beltoise R				
Monaco GP	Pescarolo P	Pescarolo 3	Beltoise R				
Belgian GP		Pescarolo R	Beltoise 3				
Dutch GP		Pescarolo 8	Beltoise 5				
French GP		Pescarolo 5	Beltoise R				
British GP	Pescarolo C		Beltoise R				
German GP		Pescarolo 6	Beltoise R				
Austrian GP		Pescarolo 14	Beltoise 6				
Italian GP		Pescarolo R	Beltoise 3				
Canadian GP	Beltoise P	Pescarolo 7	Beltoise 8				
United States GP	Beltoise P	Pescarolo 8	Beltoise R				
Mexican GP	S	Pescarolo 9	Beltoise 5				
1971							
Argentine GP		Amon 1					
South African GP			Amon 5				
Questor GP			Amon 4				
Spanish GP		Amon P	Amon 3		Beltoise 6		
International Trophy				Amon 10	Beltoise R		
Monaco GP				Amon R	Beltoise R	Amon P	
Dutch GP				Amon C	Beltoise 9	Amon P	

Results

Year and race	Chassis number and result						
	MS120/01	MS120/02	MS120/03	MS120B/04	MS120B/05	MS120B/06	MS120C/07
1971							
French GP				Amon P	Beltoise 7	Amon 5	
British GP					Beltoise 7	Amon R	
German GP				Amon P		Amon C	
Italian GP				Amon P		Amon 6	
Canadian GP					Beltoise C	Amon 10	
United States GP					Beltoise 8	Amon 12	
1972							
Argentine GP						Amon P	
South African GP						Amon 15	
Spanish GP				Amon P		Amon R	
Monaco GP				Amon 6		Amon P	
Belgian GP						Amon 6	
French GP				S			Amon 3
British GP				Amon 4			Amon P/C
German GP				S			Amon 14
Austrian GP				S			Amon 5
Italian GP				P			Amon R
Canadian GP							Amon 6
United States GP							Amon 15

C=Crash; D=disqualified; NQ=non-qualifier; P=practice car only; R=retired; S=spare car not used

Repco-Brabham

BT19, BT20 and BT24

Type	BT19, BT20 and BT24
Years of construction	1965-7
Number made	BT19-1, BT20-2, BT24-3
Frame designer	Ron Tauranac
Frame	Multi tubular space frame
Front suspension	Double wishbone with outboard coil spring/damper units
Rear suspension	Lower wishbone, upper transverse link, two forward running radius arms with outboard coil spring/damper units
Engine make	Repco
Engine designer	Phil Irving
Engine type	BT19 and BT20—Type 620, BT24—Type 740
Engine capacity	2994cc
Cylinders	8 in 90° Vee formation
Bore and stroke	88.9mm x 60.3mm
Valves per cylinder	1 inlet per cylinder in Vee, 1 exhaust per cylinder laterally (reversed in 740 with 4 valves per cylinder)
Carburation	Lucas port fuel injection
Ignition	Coil and distributor
Sparking plugs	1 centrally placed 14mm plug per cylinder
Camshafts per bank	1 overhead (2 in 740)
Gearbox	Hewland HD5 for first three races in 1966 Hewland DG300 for all other appearances except Dutch GP 1967 when BT24 used a Hewland FT200
Brakes	Outboard discs

Repco-Brabham BT19/F1-1-65 and BT20/F1-2-66   The 1966 Brabhams sandwich the Lotus of Jim Clark. Brabham maintained his position to win the Dutch GP

Jack Brabham won the World Championship of drivers in 1959 and 1960. No new horizons seemed left for him to conquer until he conceived the idea of constructing and driving his own car in the 1962 series of races. Although the World Championship had been in existence for twelve years, he was the first man to drive cars of his own manufacture, at least on a businesslike basis. Brabham seemed to be the only British constructor to learn a lesson from the start of the 1½ litre Formula, when a whole year was lost to Ferrari as no competitive car was ready. Brabham therefore made his preparations well in advance of the 1966 season.

Probably by accident, he realised that domination of a Formula is not achieved by using a proprietary engine which is easily available to one's competitors. For financial reasons, this simple truism has been forgotten by today's manufacturers.

Probably on purpose, he did not pitch his technical sights too high. The result was spectacular, for the World Championship was won for the first two years of the 3 litre Formula. Only three cars were used in 1966, although Hulme used an older, Coventry-Climax engined car earlier in the year. All the new cars won races, which is a tribute in itself to the excellence of workmanship that went into these splendid machines.

BT19 F1-1-65 Early in 1965, Brabham commissioned Ron Tauranac to design and build a car to take the 1½ litre Coventry-Climax sixteen-cylinder engine. This engine was never released to manufacturers as the FWMV eight-cylinder engine remained competitive until the end of the previous Formula. Therefore Brabham had available a chassis large enough to take the 3 litre Repco engine when it was ready. This chassis was of conventional Brabham design with a tubular space frame and standard wishbone and coil spring suspension. Everything was designed with lightness and ease of maintenance in view.

For the first season, Repco also went for simplicity. This Australian firm of engine manufacturers used standard car parts wherever possible, such as an Oldsmobile cylinder block and Daimler con rods. The power was never much over 300 BHP, compared with BRM or Ferrari who quoted higher outputs. Brabham realised that the crux of the problem was the minimum weight limit applied to cars by the rules. Accordingly he built his cars right down to that limit, which more than overcame any

power deficiency he may have had—although it was said at the time that horse for horse Brabham's were always stronger than anyone else's !

The first car was ready for the very first race to the new Formula in 1966—the South African GP—and was the only full 3 litre one there. It was fitted with the old Hewland HD5 gearbox which was a little frail for the power of the engine, the new DG300 gearbox not being ready until the Monaco GP. Consequently Brabham could not drive the car to its full potential; nevertheless he led the race until an unfortunate spin and subsequent failure to restart. Back in Europe, the Syracuse GP was a similar sad story as a fuel injection metering unit failed after only three laps.

It was getting close to the start of the proper season by now and Brabham began to get serious. All the major teams were represented at the International Trophy race at Silverstone where Brabham served notice of his serious intentions by being fastest in practice and leading the race from start to finish. He was challenged by Surtees in his Ferrari but only at the start of the race. So it was on to Monaco and the nitty gritty. The beginning was inauspicious for an engine was blown in practice, and in the race the gearbox failed early on. The potential was also hidden at Spa. All season Brabham was second to the Ferraris in sheer flat out speed. This was particularly evident at Spa, Rheims and Monza. He finished a distant fourth in the Belgian GP when Rindt had an enormous spin in pouring rain just in front of him.

Fortune began to change and at Rheims Brabham recorded the first ever win in a World Championship race by a man driving a car of his own making. Hulme had his new car for the French GP and this helped Brabham in his efforts. Following the win at Rheims the team settled down to a period of domination rare in Grand Prix racing. An easy first place in the British GP was followed by wins in the Dutch and German GPs, and the World Championship for 1966 was virtually over.

With the Championship won, much of the incentive was gone and the rest of the season was rather an anti-climax. In the Italian GP, after Brabham had led for the first few laps, a timing box cover fell off and the oil was lost. As F1-1-65 was not taken to the United States the last race of the season was the Gold Cup at Oulton Park where a win was achieved, albeit against a very small field.

Their successful 1966 season must have exceeded the team's

wildest dreams when almost everything went right. Competition is always hard at work, however, and Brabham realised he would have to build a new car, to be named the BT24. Until this was ready, the old ones had to be used.

At the Monaco GP, it had been intended that F1-1-65 should be there purely as a spare but, when Brabham blew the interim Repco engine in F1-1-66 in practice, the new Repco Type 740 was installed in F1-1-65 for the race. As the other firms were rapidly becoming competitive, it was realised that a lot more engine power would be needed for the 1967 season. The new engine was purely Repco, with the standard block and con rods being discarded as they were not strong enough to withstand the stresses of an increased power output. This engine was quoted at the outset as developing 325 BHP at 8300 RPM, as opposed to the 310 BHP at 7100 RPM of the old one. In spite of the increased strength built into the engine, a con rod broke at the start of the race, so the all-night work of the mechanics installing the engine had been in vain.

Fears concerning the opposition were more than fulfilled in the Dutch GP where Brabham was easily overtaken by Clark in the new Lotus 49. Nevertheless a second place was still useful in an outdated car. Brabham's new car was now ready and Hulme raced the BT19 in the Belgian GP, but he was forced to retire when the oil scavenge system failed. This proved to be the last World Championship race for the F1-1-65, although it was kept as a spare. Gardner used it in the Gold Cup Race, retiring with ignition failure; and in its final appearance in the Spanish GP Brabham had a steady rather than spectacular race into third place. So perhaps the most famous of all Brabham cars went into retirement with a magnificent record of six first places—while not the most ever achieved by one machine, it is certainly well in the top bracket.

BT20 F1-1-66 This car, although numbered first in the series, was actually the last to appear. The 1966 World Championship was already won before the car was seen in public when Brabham used it in practice for the Italian GP. As F1-1-65 had had a long season, F1-1-66 was taken to the USA for Brabham to use. It looked as if the tradition was going to be maintained for, when Bandini retired the Ferrari, Brabham inherited the lead; but a cam follower failed and jammed a camshaft. In Mexico, after an engine

had failed in practice, Brabham followed Surtees all the way in the race to gain the car's first placing.

At the start of 1967 it was used as Brabham's No 1 car until his BT24 was ready. For the South African GP, which that year counted towards the World Championship, the 'interim' Repco engine should have been available. This had the new cylinder head with four camshafts and the exhaust ports in the Vee of the engine, mated to the Oldsmobile block. However, it was not ready until the Oulton Park Spring Cup, and the old engine was used. After running second for a long while, Brabham suffered an intermittent engine malady which later cured itself so that he finished sixth. The Race of Champions was no better, with many problems showing up, but the new engine gave Brabham a win in the Spring Cup. It was apparent that the car's Grand Prix days were nearly over when it was easily outpaced by Parkes in the International Trophy race. It appeared at the Monaco GP, but blew an engine in practice and was not used in the race.

The BT24s were now ready, so F1-1-66 was pensioned off and sold to John Love, the Rhodesian driver. He used it in the South African National races which were run to Formula 1 regulations. The car replaced Love's ex-Tasman Cooper-Coventry-Climax which he had raced successfully for several years. Helped by sponsorship from PECO, Love had enormous success with the car. He had easy wins in the Natal Winter Trophy, the Governor General's Cup—which was stopped after fourteen laps when Luki Botha's BT11 crashed—and the van Riebeck Trophy. A pit-stop in the Rand Spring Trophy meant that Love finished third, but he was first again in the Pat Fairfield Trophy and Rhodesian GP. He was the first native driver to finish in the 1968 South African GP, in ninth place. However, in the National races he was forced to retire in the first of the 1968 series, the Cape South Easter Trophy, the cause being engine failure.

It was obvious now that F1-1-66 was a bit tired. As some of the other drivers had more competitive cars (Tingle and van Rooyen had bought BT24s) Love, sponsored by a tobacco firm, bought a Lotus 49. The BT20 was sold to Peter de Klerk who was an underrated driver. He first raced the car towards the end of the 1968 season, taking a fourth place in the Rand Spring Trophy and competing in the Rhodesian GP. De Klerk had his final drive in the car in the 1969 South African GP when he finished ninth. It was then sold to ex-driver Jack Holme for Clive Puzey, who previously drove the extensively modified ex-Parnell (aren't they all?), ex-Gary Hocking Lotus 18/21. Puzey had several drives in the BT20. It was also used once by his team-mate John Rowe, who was disqualified in the 1969 Rand Autumn Trophy for not coming under starter's orders.

De Klerk drove the car again in 1970, but failed to be classified in the Rand Summer Trophy. Subsequently it was driven by a new member of Jack Holme's team—Bruce van der Merwe. In spite of a fifth place in the Natal Winter Trophy, the car was now very near the end of its racing days and was taken away to honourable retirement in Donnington Park.

BT20 F1-2-66   In contrast with F1-1-66, the second car of the series spent all its racing life based in Europe. It first appeared at the 1966 French GP, driven by Hulme, when it finished third. The car differed from the BT19 in having a space frame constructed entirely of round tubes, whereas the older car used a combination of round and oval ones. Also, the exhaust pipes surrounded the upper radius arm instead of winding outside it. To reach third in its first race was outstanding and, to emphasise the point, Hulme finished an easy second to Brabham in the British GP.

While Hulme was being blooded in Grand Prix racing, his car was almost always tried by Brabham in practice to make sure it was right. As Brabham's car was going so well, it was obvious that more effort should be put into it as the World Championship was well within his grasp. Hulme consequently suffered retirements in the Dutch and German GPs, with ignition and engine trouble respectively, having had promising drives in each race.

In the Italian GP it was Hulme's turn to uphold the Brabham banner, as the boss retired early on. Hulme was in the leading group all the way, but was beaten for sheer speed by the Ferraris and finished third. After a second place to the team leader at Oulton Park, Hulme retired with oil pressure, or rather lack of it, in the United States GP. However the season ended on a strong note when, after a poor start, he came up the field well, finishing third.

Many cars suffered from fuel vapourisation problems at the first race in 1967—the South African GP. Hulme's was no exception; he was leading the race at the time, and after the fuel pump had been packed with dry ice he salvaged fourth place from the wreckage. There were three pre-season races in

Britain that year and Hulme competed in them all, with two retirements and a second place, in the Spring Cup, to show for his efforts. These results were not to be taken too seriously, unlike the Monaco GP which was to follow. To everyone's surprise Hulme took the lead on the second lap and held it to the end, winning by over a lap from Hill in the Lotus. As the BT24 was not quite ready, Hulme had to use the BT20 for the Dutch GP; it again went well for him and he finished behind Brabham in third place. Like F1-1-66, this car had also served its time as far as the factory was concerned and it was sold to Guy Ligier to replace his Type 81 Cooper.

Ligier was one of several drivers of the time who pottered round the circuits of Europe. They always filled the back of the grid, were usually lapped many times in the race and were much reviled by the press for clogging up the circuits. But they certainly enjoyed themselves and, as far as the historian is concerned, added much interest to the scene. Ligier first drove F1-2-66 to tenth place in the British GP, four laps behind the leader. In the German GP, however, he managed to gain a World Championship point when everyone else retired so that he automatically finished sixth—and last. After a couple of retirements, the finishing line was achieved again in Mexico, this time in eleventh place.

Ligier stepped down a league in 1968 when he formed the Inter Sport team with Jo Schlesser to race Formula 2 McLaren M4A cars. He sold the BT20 to the long-time Brabham protagonist, Charles Vogele, for Silvio Moser to race. Moser had been around for a long while in Formula 3 and Formula 2, driving a variety of Brabhams and the rare BWA, and this was his first sortie into the top flight. Considering how competitive he had been in the lesser Formulas, it was surprising he never made the grade in Formula 1. After a retirement in the Race of Champions he finished seventh and last in the International Trophy. At Monaco he was unlucky not to qualify for the start, as he was faster in practice than two of the officially invited starters. Moser had his best race in the BT20 at Zandvoort, finishing fifth after an excellent drive in an outdated motor. But this was the beginning of the end. At Spa he had two long pit-stops with

Repco-Brabham BT24/2 The 1967 car differed from the previous cars only in detail—Hulme in the French GP

90

gearbox trouble and the season ended when he failed to qualify for the start in either the German or Italian GPs.

BT24/1 After the domination Brabham had achieved in 1966 there seemed no real urgency about the preparation of the new 1967 cars and the first one, BT24/1, appeared at the Dutch GP. This proved to be ominous for this race also marked the first showing of the new Lotus 49, with the Cosworth DFV engine, which was to become such a thorn in the side of Brabham. The new Brabham, very similar to the previous year, was a little narrower as the fuel tanks had been situated in the multi-tube space frame, instead of outside it. It was, of course, fitted with the new Repco Type 740 engine. For this race only, as an experiment, it used the much lighter Hewland FT200 Formula 2 gearbox, but at the Belgian GP the DG300 Formula 1 gearbox replaced it. Brabham did not intend to race the car at Zandvoort and merely tested it in practice.

In Belgium the main fault revealed itself and the sad thing was that nothing could be done about it. Brabham, in spite of the low weight of the cars, was at last being out-performed by another contender. But there was also some good news—the more powerful cars were not reliable. Nevertheless Brabham must have seen very early on that, unless Clark and Hill retired, he and Hulme must resign themselves to third and fourth places. This was the situation at Spa, although it was all a bit academic as Brabham had to retire the car when the oil scavenge pump failed. It was the last time that Brabham was to retire from a Formula 1 race in 1967.

The Brabhams had wins in the German, French and Canadian GPs after both the Lotuses retired. They also won the Oulton Park Gold Cup race when Lotus did not enter. If one adds second places in Italy and Mexico, when only one Lotus retired, the season could be proudly described as a good one and the World Championship for Manufacturers was easily won.

It was obvious that a new car was desperately needed and, after retiring from the South African GP, Brabham wasted no time at all. He sold the BT24 straight away to STP (South Africa) for the well-known saloon-car driver Basil van Rooyen to drive in South African national Formula 1 races. Van Rooyen's titanic duels in various Fords with Koos Swanepoel will long be remembered in South Africa.

Van Rooyen received his car in time for the 1968 Rand Autumn Trophy in March and, after a couple of retirements, settled into his groove which strangely paralleled that in Europe the previous year. John Love had purchased a Lotus 49 and if that kept going he won; if not, then van Rooyen usually won. So it was that van Rooyen won the Bulawayo 100 and Natal Winter Trophy races, and had seconds in the South Africa Republic Festival Trophy, Rand Winter Trophy and Rand Spring Trophy races.

By the end of the year van Rooyen saw that he could never hope to beat Love with the BT24, so he purchased a McLaren M7A. The Brabham was sold to Gordon Henderson, who had not raced in Formula 1 since 1962, but he buckled down to the task and achieved a few minor places. At the end of 1969 he tried to prolong the life of the BT24 by fitting a Cosworth DFV engine, but it did not work very well and the car became more and more unreliable until Henderson gave up the struggle in mid-1970. Yet another Brabham kept going for a much longer period than most racing cars—they really were very strong motor cars.

BT24/2 Hulme, in common with Brabham, was in no great hurry for his new car, having won with the old one at Monaco. But it was ready in time for the French GP, which was held at the Mickey Mouse circuit to end all Mickey Mouse circuits—the Bugatti course at Le Mans. It was described at the time as the Grand Prix de Car Parks. It suited the Brabhams, however, and as the others dropped out so Hulme moved up the field into second place. Apart from the head gasket blowing in the Italian GP when he was in the leading group, Hulme had a 100 per cent finishing record in Grand Prix. With a win in the German GP; seconds in the French, British and Canadian GPs, and thirds in the United States and Mexican GPs, Hulme just won the World Championship from his boss.

The Mexican GP was Hulme's last race for Brabham as he had decided to leave the Australian team. As a New Zealander he wished to join up with Bruce McLaren's team for 1968 and, in fact, stayed with them right through to 1974. Nevertheless it is his partnership with Brabham which will be chiefly remembered as one of the great ones of motor racing. Fangio, Farina and Fagioli; Fangio and Moss; Hawthorn and Collins; Moss and Brooks; Brabham and McLaren are all great partnerships, and

Brabham and Hulme certainly ranks with these.

Hulme's replacement for 1968 was the dynamic young Austrian driver Jochen Rindt, who pedalled the Coopers so fast. On the surface this looked a good move for, while Coopers were on the way down, Brabham were expecting the new four camshaft Repco engine as a match for the Cosworth. Sadly it did not come up to expectations and for Rindt it was to be a wasted year.

The BT26 was not ready immediately and Rindt had one drive in BT24/2 before it was sold; true to form, in the South African GP, he finished third behind—who else—Clark and Hill.

The car was sold to Team Gunston, a South African cigarette firm, for Sam Tingle to drive as a replacement for his old LDS. Sam, like his team mate John Love, had been around for a long, long time and started his racing career as far back as 1947. He had known great success, winning the South African Championship on three occasions, but was now in the twilight of his career. That does not mean that he was not quick, because he was. In South Africa only van Rooyen, Love and Charlton were faster and in 1968 Tingle was rewarded with second places in the Natal Winter Trophy and Rhodesian GP, and thirds in the Bulawayo 100, South Africa Republic Festival Trophy and False Bay 100.

Tingle retained the car in 1969. He entered for the South African World Championship round and finished eighth, with a further five second places during the year, proving that in spite of its advancing years the old car could still go well. Tingle was either very fortunate or very lucky in his choice of mechanics as his previous car, the LDS, had lasted for two years, while the LDS before that had managed six years of continuous competition. What a machine LDS/1 would make for Tom Wheatcroft's marvellous collection at Donington Park!

Tingle was planning on another season in 1970, although well into his forties. Sadly it was not to be for, in the first race of the year, he crashed. As well as wrecking the BT24, he was badly injured himself and wisely decided to hang up his driving gloves.

BT24/3 At the start of the 1969 season, a little temporising had to be done as the two existing BT24s had been sold and the BT26s were not ready. The solution was to build up a third BT24 from the spare parts which had never been needed because the cars had been so reliable. Rindt drove the BT24/3 at the Spanish and Monaco GPs. In the former he retired early on with oil pressure falling, while at Monaco he made the mistake of trying to push his way past Surtees in Casino Square. What a man to try that trick on !

The car was repaired in time for the Dutch GP and, as Rindt's BT26 was ready, the BT24 was loaned to Gurney who had a miserable time in the pouring rain. He spun a couple of times and eventually, with a sticking throttle as well, he quietly gave up in the pits. The car was used for a little longer as a spare and hired to the Caltex Racing Team for the underrated German, Kurt Ahrens, to drive into twelfth place in the German GP.

As the third BT26 had now been completed, the BT24 was sold off to demon wheeler-dealer Frank Williams, who was going to prepare it for the Tasman series of races. So the car was fitted with small tanks and Cosworth DFV engine for the brief antipodean races, but the plans never came to fruition. Williams then fitted pannier tanks to carry sufficient fuel for the longer races and sold it. The purchaser was the little Swiss driver, Silvio Moser, who wanted to replace his no longer competitive BT20.

Moser had a full season with the car, not setting the world alight but no doubt enjoying himself. His best placing of the year was in the United States GP when he got his first point of the season in the Championship. He was lying sixth again in Mexico, in his last race with the car, when a fuel leak caused him to retire from the competition. So the car was sold, to be replaced by the unique Formula 1 Bellasi.

One cannot but admire the way Brabham went about his work in the 1966 and 1967 seasons. He was lucky in that the other manufacturers initially failed to appreciate the key to the 3 litre Formula. BRM were far too complex and heavy with the H16. In 1966 Lotus had no 3 litre engine at all worth talking about. Cooper and Honda were far too heavy, and Ferrari had lost his sense of direction. This left Brabham with everything in his favour. He had two of the best drivers, who knitted together with the mechanics to form the most harmonious team. He had a reliable engine with adequate power, which was only available to his team. He had a strong and reliable car, which was very light and held the road as well as, if not better than, his competitors. His reward was the World Championship.

It was almost the same story in 1967. Lotus started to catch up, but were too far behind when they made their effort as late as the Dutch GP with a brand new car. The others had not learnt the lessons of 1966. The reward was another World Championship for Brabham.

The most remarkable thing was the low cost of these successes; in comparative terms the 1966 World Championship was probably the cheapest ever. But there is a disease common to almost all World Championship winners—that of thinking the others cannot catch up. In fairness to Brabham it was not entirely his fault, for his cars still cornered as quickly as anyone's. The trouble was that the engine was at last overtaken in the lightness/power stakes by Cosworth. After a season Brabham was forced into using the engine, in common with most other constructors. The balance of power had shifted.

Results

Year and race	Chassis number and result					
1966	F1-1-65	F1-1-66	F1-2-66	BT24/1	BT24/2	BT24/3
South African GP	Brabham R					
Syracuse GP	Brabham R					
International Trophy	Brabham 1					
Monaco GP	Brabham R					
Belgian GP	Brabham 4					
French GP	Brabham 1		Hulme 3			
	Hulme P		Brabham P			
British GP	Brabham 1		Hulme 2			
Dutch GP	Brabham 1		Hulme R			
			Brabham P			
German GP	Brabham 1		Hulme R			
			Brabham P			
Italian GP	Brabham R	Brabham P	Hulme 3			
Gold Cup Race	Brabham 1		Hulme 2			
			Brabham P			
United States GP		Brabham R	Hulme R			
			Brabham P			

Results

Year and race	Chassis number and result					
	F1-1-65	F1-1-66	F1-2-66	BT24/1	BT24/2	BT24/3
1966						
Mexican GP		Brabham 2	Hulme 3			
1967						
South African GP		Brabham 6	Hulme 4			
Race of Champions		Brabham 9	Hulme R			
Spring Trophy		Brabham 1	Hulme 2			
International Trophy		Brabham 2	Hulme R			
Monaco GP	Brabham R	Brabham P	Hulme 1			
Dutch GP	Brabham 2	S	Hulme 3	Brabham P		
Belgian GP	Hulme R		S	Brabham R		
	Brabham P					
Natal Winter Trophy		Love 1				
French GP				Brabham 1	Hulme 2	
British GP			Ligier 10	Brabham 4	Hulme 2	
Governor Gen. Cup		Love 1				
German GP	Brabham P		Ligier 6	Brabham 2	Hulme 1	
Canadian GP				Brabham 1	Hulme 2	
Van Riebeck Trophy		Love 1				
Italian GP			Ligier R	Brabham 2	Hulme R	
Gold Cup Race	Gardner R			Brabham 1		
United States GP			Ligier R	Brabham 5	Hulme 3	
Rand Spring Trophy		Love 3				
Mexican GP			Ligier 11	Brabham 2	Hulme 3	

Results

Year and race	Chassis number and result					
1967	F1-1-65	F1-1-66	F1-2-66	BT24/1	BT24/2	BT24/3
Pat Fairfield Trophy		Love 1				
Spanish GP	Brabham 3					
Rhodesian GP		Love 1				
1968						
South African GP		Love 9		Brabham R	Rindt 3	
Cape South Easter Trophy		Love R				
Race of Champions			Moser R			
Rand Autumn Trophy				Rooyen R	Tingle C	
Coronation 100				Rooyen R	Tingle 7	
International Trophy			Moser 7			
Bulawayo 100				Rooyen 1	Tingle 3	
Spanish GP						Rindt R
Monaco GP			Moser NQ			Rindt C
SA Republic Fest. Trophy				Rooyen 2	Tingle 3	
Dutch GP			Moser 5			Gurney R
Natal Winter Trophy				Rooyen 1	Tingle 2	
French GP						Brabham P
Border 100				Rooyen C	Tingle 4	
British GP			Moser 11			Rindt P
Rand Winter Trophy				Rooyen 2	Tingle 4	
German GP			Moser NQ			Ahrens 12
False Bay 100				Rooyen R	Tingle 3	

Results

Year and race	Chassis number and result					
1968	F1-1-65	F1-1-66	F1-2-66	BT24/1	BT24/2	BT24/3
Italian GP			Moser NQ			
Rand Spring Trophy		de Klerk 4		Rooyen 2	Tingle 5	
Rhodesian GP		de Klerk ?		Rooyen R	Tingle 2	
1969						
Cape South Easter Trophy		Puzey 5			Tingle 2	
South African GP		de Klerk 9			Tingle 8	
Coronation 100		Puzey R		Henderson C	Tingle R	
Rand Autumn Trophy		Rowe D		Henderson R	Tingle NS	
Bulawayo 100		Puzey ?		Henderson ?	Tingle ?	
Monaco GP						Moser R
SA Republic Fest Trophy		Puzey R		Henderson 6	Tingle 2	
Dutch GP						Moser R
Natal Winter Trophy				Henderson R	Tingle 2	
French GP						Moser 7
Border 100				Henderson 7	Tingle 6	
General's Cup					Tingle 4	
Rand Winter Trophy				Henderson 5	Tingle 2	
Gold Cup Race						Moser 4
False Bay 100				Henderson R	Tingle 4	
Italian GP						Moser R
Rhodesian GP					Tingle 2	
Canadian GP						Moser C

Results

Year and race	Chassis number and result					
1969	F1-1-65	F1-1-66	F1-2-66	BT24/1	BT24/2	BT24/3
Rand Spring Trophy				Henderson NS	Tingle 2	
United States GP						Moser 6
Mexican GP						Moser 11/R
1970						
Cape South Easter Trophy				Henderson D	Tingle C	
Rand Summer Trophy		de Klerk 8		Henderson P		
Coronation 100		der Merwe 6		Henderson R		
SA Republic Fest. Trophy		der Merwe 11		Henderson P		
Natal Winter Trophy		der Merwe 5				
General's Cup		der Merwe 5				
Rand Winter Trophy		der Merwe R		Robertson R		
False Bay 100		der Merwe R		Robertson R		
Rhodesian GP		der Merwe R				
Rand Spring Trophy		der Merwe 3				
Welkom 100		der Merwe 3				

C= Crash ; D=disqualified ; NQ=non-qualifier ; P=practice car only ; R=retired ; S=spare car not used

Shadow

DN1 and DN3

Type	DN1 and DN3
Years of construction	1973-4
Number made	DN1-6, DN3-5
Frame designer	Tony Southgate
Frame	Monocoque chassis to cockpit, engine forms rear of chassis, deformable structures fitted in cockpit area
Front suspension	Double wishbones with outboard coil spring/ damper units
Rear suspension	Lower wishbone, upper transverse link, single forward running radius arm (2 in DN3) with outboard coil spring/damper units
Engine make	Cosworth
Engine designer	Keith Duckworth with Mike Costin
Engine type	DFV
Engine capacity	2993cc
Cylinders	8 in 90° Vee formation
Bore and stroke	85.7mm x 64.8mm
Valves per cylinder	2 inlet per cylinder in Vee, 2 exhaust per cylinder laterally
Carburation	Lucas port fuel injection
Ignition	Lucas OPUS system
Sparking plugs	1 centrally placed 10mm plug per cylinder
Camshafts	2 overhead
Gearbox	Hewland TL200
Brakes	Outboard discs

Although the Americans have types of motor racing which are all their own, there can be no doubt that when it comes to the crunch Grand Prix Racing is the thing. This explains why the Americans organise a World Championship round and why periodic sallies are made into Formula 1 construction. After the unfortunate flight of the Eagle a hiatus developed, as British-made cars dominated Grand Prix racing and made serious inroads into American single-seater track racing. So it was with interest that the fans heard of the intention of the Shadow team to enter Grand Prix racing in 1973. Controlled by Don Nicholls and sponsored by Universal Oil Products, Nicholls Advanced Vehicle Systems entered CanAm sports car races in 1970 with a most peculiar machine which achieved a very low profile by using 10in front wheels and 12in rears. The Shadow was always quick though rarely reliable, but at least it gave the turbo-charged Porsches something to beat in the later years of the class.

When Shadow decided to contest Formula 1 races they engaged Alan Rees as team manager. Rees had been a driver himself in the mid-1960s with the very successful Roy Winklemann Racing Team Formula 2 Brabhams, and later became the 'R' in the name 'March,' although he eventually left the team. The designer was Tony Southgate of BRM fame—a fact which showed in the car. He was used to the smoothness of the V12 engine and was surprised by the roughness of the Cosworth DFV which Shadow used. This was the age of the British standard kit car and Shadow joined the club with a car which was basically the same as the others but with detail differences.

The first year can only be described as disastrous as Shadow crashed their way around Europe leaving trails of wreckage behind them. The drivers were not entirely to blame for the cars were just not structurally sound enough and things kept falling off. Luckily Shadow were not discouraged and the second year was much better. By the third year the cars were fully competitive— even, on occasions, setting the pace—which all goes to show how rapidly progress can be made nowadays.

DN1 1A The car appeared for the first time at the 1973 South African GP and right away was in trouble with vibration. The chassis was of monocoque construction with the engine forming

Shadow DN1/6A   Its finest hour—Jack Oliver leads the 1973 Canadian GP

the rear part of the chassis. The problem was that the front engine mounts started to pull out of the chassis, and this was solved by fitting longer bolts. Southgate did not follow his Type 180 BRM practice—which he was never able fully to develop—of placing the radiators at the rear of the car; instead they were placed slanting backwards at the front of the engine compartment. The chassis bulged in the cockpit area for the fuel cells to be accommodated, together with the deformable polyurethane foam. The suspension followed standard Southgate practice, including the steeply angled spring dampers at the front.

Appointed to drive 1A was that follower of duff cars, Jack Oliver. One of the quickest still around, he was probably getting a bit disillusioned with Grand Prix racing by this time. As with Trevor Taylor, this can show in trying too hard, although in 1973 Oliver was certainly more sinned against than sinning. However he got no chance to sin in the South African GP for his engine stopped working fairly early in the race.

The cars returned to England for the International Trophy race at Silverstone and, needless to say, had their engine mountings strengthened. Oliver again lost interest early on when his clutch failed at the start. The problem recurred in practice for the Spanish GP, but in the race it was overheating that led to retirement when he was not very well placed.

In 1973 the Belgian GP was held at Zolder and the drivers were all upset about the track surface which had only just been relaid. It began to break up under the enormous stresses placed on it by the cornering power of the modern, sticky, very wide tyres. Oliver was caught out by this and crashed, bending the chassis sufficiently to cause the car to be written off.

DN1 2A The second car was entrusted to George Follmer who had been with Shadow on and off since the beginning. He had no previous experience of Grand Prix racing, but found no real difficulty in adjusting to it after CanAm racing where the cars are virtually two-seater Grand Prix cars and somewhat faster in a straight line. He had, for instance, driven the turbo-charged Porsche 917 which was the first road racing car to develop over 1000 BHP. So the mere 400 of the Cosworth engine must have seemed very small beer, but it was worse than that at Follmer's first race as it would not pull properly. Nevertheless he did finish and, because the others retired, was classified as sixth.

Follmer had a much better drive in the International Trophy, when the engine behaved itself, and he took another sixth place. The real surprise was the Spanish GP where, admittedly profiting by other retirements, Follmer finished a fine third. The fact that the others retired in no way diminished Follmer's efforts as he was still on the same lap as the winner at the end of the race.

At the Belgian GP Follmer started off the shunting habit when he crashed in the practice session and kinked the monocoque. The machine was straightened out for the race, but then the throttles stuck open and he was off the road again, this time just into the sand. Worse was to come on the streets of Monte Carlo when, in practice, Merzario and Follmer had a coming together. At this time both men were 'hard chargers' and it is difficult to decide who was to blame. The result was one Shadow bent, with no wheels—such was the damage that the car was unreparable and it was written off.

DN1 3A This car remains unique among the Grand Prix Shadows to date in that it is the only one sold for a private owner to race. The driver in question was Graham Hill who, with sponsorship from Embassy cigarettes, was setting up his own Grand Prix team for the first time. The car was ready, but completely untested, in time for the 1973 Spanish GP, and it was no surprise when it retired with brake failure. The car had been assembled not by the Shadow works but by Hill's own mechanics to the Shadow specifications, using a Shadow monocoque chassis. Following the Spanish race, Hill managed to do some testing and sort the car out for the Belgian GP. Although he had to stop to have a loose plug lead fixed early in the race, he managed a ninth place at the end.

The Monaco GP really showed up the DN1 for the disaster it was—the bumps and swerves of the tiny circuit almost ripped Hill's car apart. As well as suffering a puncture, the monocoque chassis fractured and the rear suspension pulled away from the chassis at another point which caused the rear wheels to steer as well as the front. Hill—very wisely, one feels—gave up.

It was therefore no surprise when the car turned up for the next race considerably strengthened in the chassis department. Even so, Hill had another unsatisfactory race as his throttle slides jammed at the start and he then had to retire with ignition

failure. Things were slowly beginning to untangle themselves, however. If Hill had learnt nothing else during his long period of racing, he had learnt how to sort out a car. In the French GP the car was much better and Hill had a very good race, managing to get as high as eighth before vibration set in and he dropped down to tenth.

The eventful first year of the Shadows continued to Silverstone where all three cars were involved in accidents on the first lap. As is well known in England—since the incident is shown on television whenever motor racing is mentioned—Scheckter, in one of his very early drives for McLaren, spun at the end of the first lap. Many cars were involved in the ensuing fracas, including Follmer and Hill. Graham was singularly fortunate, the only damage to the car being a broken wishbone which had been repaired by the time the race was restarted, but the car started to crack up again and the whole front sub-frame began to pull away from the chassis.

At Zandvoort it was the engine that caused the problems when it started to lose water, so that Hill had to make many stops to be replenished. In Germany he had a quiet drive for a change, but the bumps of the 'Ring twisted the chassis somewhat. This was not apparent until the team raced in Austria, where one of the radius rods pushed itself into the chassis.

These last three races had shown the car reliable and finishing each time, but Hill had had enough of Shadows. It was replaced by a Lola and 3A was given to the cigarette firm for advertising purposes. It really is remarkable, when so much fuss is made over circuit safety, barriers, chain-link fencing and so on, that someone with Hill's experience would drive a car as prone to major mechanical or structural failure as was the DN1 shadow. Considering all the incidents of 1973, it is quite surprising that none of the drivers was badly hurt. At least the deformable structure bit—and that is the important part, from a safety angle—was excellently constructed and must have been the reason why the various accidents were not more serious.

DN1 4A When a new model is brought out, a small series of chassis are built; so that, following Oliver's crash in 1A, the team were able to use the suspension from three of its wheels on the new car. They also used several other bits and had 4A ready in time for the Monaco GP. Apart from a bump on the first lap, which tore off a nose fin and slightly upset the handling, Oliver had a quiet race and his first finish of the season in tenth place.

In the Swedish GP, the car had a major structural failure when a wishbone mounting pulled out of the chassis and Oliver nearly lost a wheel. Only a single lap was completed in France, Britain and Holland: in France the clutch packed up, while in Britain Oliver had a crash with Lauda right at the start of the race. The car could have been repaired in time for the restart after Scheckter's crash, but there was trouble about it being re-scrutineered and the mechanics finished five laps too late. At Zandvoort, having managed to complete the first lap, Oliver crashed on the first corner of the second.

It took until the Austrian GP to repair the car, but it was done well and for the last time, as it was not crashed again. In Austria it was a fuel leak that caused Oliver's early departure from the race. Italy saw a red letter day in the life of 4A, it being the second and last time that the car finished a race. This was because Oliver did not drive it again—indeed it was used only once more when the popular Brian Redman had a drive for the team in the United States GP. Following a stop for a jammed throttle slide, Redman was disqualified for using outside assistance to restart. So the car departed from the scene unlamented. Apparently it is still retained at the Shadow factory—perhaps it does have a certain sentimental value.

DN1 5A   After Follmer crashed 2A in practice for the Monaco GP, there was no spare for him to drive in the race and the team had to hurry to build up a new car ready for the Swedish GP. This car was crashed even before the start of its first race. It was straightened, although perhaps not completely as in the race Follmer had to stop with an overheating tyre and finished fourteenth.

A further series of failures followed with a retirement in France, involvement in the first lap incident in Britain and a crash in Germany when badly placed. In between all this was a desultory tenth place in Holland. Finally reliability arrived and Follmer finished the last three races of the year, albeit low down.

Although 1973 had been dreadful from the point of view of reliability, the Shadow team learnt from their mistakes. While they did not win a race the next year, the car was infinitely better and much more competitive. Meanwhile 5A had but one more appearance to make—in the 1974 Argentine GP. The DN3 was not ready and Jarier used it, only to retire with a failed wheel bearing.

DN1 6A   The last model in the DN1 series was the only one to differ in any great detail from the others. It had a modified rear suspension with two radius arms instead of the previous one. It appeared in time for the Dutch GP although it was not used. When Oliver crashed his usual car, he had to use 6A in the German GP and had one of his best drives of the season to finish eighth. Now it was Follmer's turn; Oliver's car had been repaired, but Follmer's was wrecked, so in Austria he tried the new one. In the race, he was plagued by a failure of the ignition system and had to give up.

For the Italian round of the Championship the car had the wheelbase extended by means of a lengthened gearbox bell housing. It was tested in practice by Oliver who used it in the Canadian GP. This was a very confused race and the result still bears anomalies which will probably never be sorted out. The start was very wet but the track dried out so that the drivers had to call at the pits for dry-weather tyres. While this was happening there was an accident elsewhere and, to make confusion worse confounded, the course car escorting the drivers round while the wreckage was being cleared up started out in front of the wrong car. The rules say that the cars should line up behind the course car in an incident of this type. So, when it started in front of the fourth or fifth car instead of the leader, the first three or four cars gained, in effect, a whole lap lead over the rest. Luckily these included Oliver, who actually led the race for a while and, although he was later overtaken by Fittipaldi and Revson, he got a third place. This enabled the team to head the Williams and Surtees teams in the Manufacturer's Championship—no mean feat in their first year.

In the United States GP it was back down the field again after Oliver had a rear wheel replaced and suffered a loose front wheel as well. The end was near and the car was used only once more—by Jarier in the Argentine GP, when the DN1 ended its Formula 1 career by crashing into Revson who was driving the new DN3 at the time.

It was a fitting end.

As the DN1 reached the end of its violent career, the DN3 was being made ready. It varied from the old car only in detail, the main differences being in strength and road-holding, but the effects were startling. From the rear of the grid the cars shot to the front and no major chassis fault occurred all season. The team was changed completely. While George Follmer was certainly a trier, it was obvious he would never be one of the real front runners. Likewise Jack Oliver was now at the stage where he had been involved with too many Grand Prix failures ever to reap the reward of his talent. In their place the team signed Peter Revson and Jean-Pierre Jarier. Revson was one of the latest developing Grand Prix drivers one can recall. He had a season in Formula 1 way back in 1964, driving a Lotus 24, and had struck everyone by his lack of talent. But many years of CanAm and other exciting forms of racing had transformed him, and his 1973 season with McLaren had been a revelation. He had won two Grands Prix and was without doubt one of the finest Grand Prix drivers of the day. So it was with great relief that Shadow heard of his imminent release from McLaren due to their signing Fittipaldi.

Jarier, known to all as Jumper, was Revson's equivalent in the 1973 Formula 2 series. Driving the March-BMW, Jarier took the close Formula 2 world apart, scoring nearly twice as many points as anyone else. Like Revson, Jarier had been around for a while without impressing, until he suddenly got the message. So Shadow were in exceedingly good heart for the start of the season.

DN3 1A   Ready for the very first race of the 1974 season, the Argentine GP, the machine was naturally handled by Revson. Like several other cars, the Shadow, by means of a spacer between the engine and gearbox, could have its wheelbase changed. It was immediately obvious that the handling of the car was vastly improved since the previous year, except on the more bumpy circuits, such as Brands Hatch and Nurburgring. After a very good practice session Revson was on the second row of the grid, but on the sprint at the start he was pushed out of the way and into the fence by Regazzoni who was driving in his usual enthusiastic manner. He also took Jarier in the DN1 Shadow 6A off the road with him, so at least the mechanics had an early night.

The car was repaired for the Brazil GP, where Revson got away safely and ran in sixth place for a while, but eventually was forced to retire with the engine overheating—a situation which had been forseen as the same thing occurred in the practice period. Back in England the car held sixth place again, but was still not too good over the bumps. In spite of this and a loss of power from the engine, it held on to its place and the first finish for a DN3.

From Brands Hatch it was straight off to South Africa for some valuable testing before the South African GP. Revson was lapping at his usual speed when, it is thought, a pin holding the front left wishbone to the upright broke, putting the car out of control and into the newly erected barrier. Sadly Revson was killed instantly. Especially poignant was the fact that the barrier was not essential at this point, there being an adequate run-off area.

From such a bright start to the season, what had the team done to deserve a blow like this?

DN3 2A   Although Jarier's car had been finished in time for the South African GP, the entry was, of course, withdrawn, both as a mark of respect to Revson and as a check against the same fault recurring. So the car's first race was the International Trophy; from the fourth row of the grid, Jarier drove well to hold off Pescarolo and finish third.

Following two relative failures when Jarier finished low down the field after pit-stops—one due to Migault running over his nose-cone and another to running out of petrol—the team came to Monte Carlo. This was Jarier's best race of the year; he was with the front runners all the time and finished a grand third. He followed this up with a fifth place in Sweden in spite of the extinguisher going off in the cockpit.

When the car arrived at Zandvoort revised front suspension and bigger brakes had been fitted, but Jarier retired early on with throttle linkage failure.

Before the next race at the very tight Dijon-Prenois circuit, Jarier drove at Le Mans where he was involved in a crash. He was not hurt badly, only spraining his wrist, but this hurt him more than he admitted or other people realised. The injury affected his control over the car, dropping him from the 'very good' to the 'good' for a while.

Shadow DN3/2A Altogether more competitive—Jarier had several good results when he had sorted the car out

In the next four races he had a couple of eighth places and two retirements when not very well placed. The only serious problem was in the British GP, when a rear suspension mounting point pulled out of the chassis, but this did not happen again.

It was a similar story in the American series—a drive shaft broke in Canada, but a tenth place was salvaged in the United States GP.

The points gained by Jarier meant that Shadow had moved ahead of March, as well as Surtees and Williams, in the Championship. As with the DN1, Shadow gained experience and learnt lessons from the DN3, and in 1975 Jarier in the new DN5 led the first race for a long period. Shadow had at last arrived.

DN3 3A   When Revson was killed, the gap in the team took some time to fill. Eventually Brian Redman, who for quite a while had been perfectly happy in sports cars and Formula 5000, was brought out of Formula 1 retirement. Redman had won the American Formula 5000 Championship in 1973 and never really settled with the Shadow team. He disliked the pressures of modern Formula 1 racing where winning is the only thing that matters. He had been out of Formula 1 for too long to be a front runner. He was honest enough to admit this and to return to his beloved Formula 5000. Redman is such a nice chap, he deserves to enjoy himself.

Nevertheless he had three races with the team in the new car. In the first he tried really hard and finished a good seventh. His hand was blistered after the constant gear changing round the tight Spanish circuit. The Shadows have always used the Formula 2 Hewland gearbox, the TL200, from a lightness point of view and, in spite of having little trouble, they were the only team to do so for a long time. Even so, Shadows have quite a heavy change mechanism. In Belgium, Redman's engine blew up with only a few laps to go, so at least he was classified as a finisher. The final race Redman drove was Monaco, but he became involved in the first-lap pile-up started by Hulme and Beltoise and was not particularly sad to be out of the rat-race.

For one race only—the Swedish GP—Shadow joined the rent-a-car system operated by certain other manufacturers and hired the promising young Swede, Bertil Roos, to drive the car. Unfortunately he never really had a chance when the gearbox failed for the only time that year.

Shadow now had the chance to sign a permanent replacement for Revson when it became known that Token were prepared to release Welshman Tom Pryce from his contract in order that he could get some drives. Pryce had been a dominating figure in Formula 3 and surprised everyone by his speed in the Token Formula 1 car. He certainly started off his career with a bang. In the Dutch GP he went for the same gap as James Hunt at the start and that was that; while in the French GP from the second row of the grid (!) he lagged a little and was pushed across the road by Reutemann into his old friend—James Hunt !

As a new chassis was now ready, Shadow put Pryce in that for the next race. They transferred into it all the bits and pieces from 3A, including the chassis number plate. This created problems because 3A, having been repaired, reappeared at Monza. By then 4A had been written off, so the easiest thing to do was to put the plate 4A on to chassis 3A. It was not until South America 1975 that 3A reacquired its proper number.

So it was 3A that Pryce drove at Monza, finishing tenth after a stop early on for a tyre change. The car was not seen again in public until 1975 when Pryce drove it twice more until his new DN5 was ready. In Argentina he was classified twelfth, suffering from transmission trouble, while in Brazil he crashed the car without injury, after having had handling problems for some time.

Like Jarier, Pryce hoped that the DN3 would be a jumping off point for him. So he was very disappointed to hear that Ronnie Peterson was being tried in the DN3 cockpit in South America, but luckily this came to nothing. Pryce then proved himself by gaining the Shadow's first victory at the 1975 Race of Champions and having a marvellous ride at the start of the Monaco GP in pouring rain.

DN3 4A   The fourth of the series was really meant to be the spare and practice car and so it was for quite a while. First seen in Monaco without being used, it was practised at various races until, at the practice for the Austrian GP, Pryce went off the road and damaged it beyond repair. A rather sad end for a car that never started in a race.

DN3 5A   The final chassis of the series was unveiled at the British GP, when Pryce drove it as a replacement for the car he had battered about in the two previous races. It carried many bits from 3A, including the chassis number plate—in fact, there never was a true chassis number plate 5A. Although Pryce finished seventh in his first race with the car, he had a lot of trouble with it slipping out of gear. This was due to the breaking of a chassis tube, causing gear linkage distortion.

Pryce had his best placing of the year in the German GP when he drove an excellent race for his first Championship point and sixth place. Following his accident in 4A in practice for the Austrian GP, he had further problems in the race when 5A was misfiring and, after that was corrected, he spun off the course, stalled and was quite unable to restart the car.

For the Italian GP it was given a rest, being used only for practice. It was back in harness for the American races, where Pryce was not really on form, but neither was the car for, with all the crashes in mid-season, it had not had any real modifications carried out on it for some time. So the season finished on a quiet note with a retirement posted in Canada due to engine failure, and a fifteenth place at Watkins Glen after stops with misfiring and a loose nose-cone.

At the close of the second season, Shadow could congratulate themselves on the ground they had covered in their invasion of the Grand Prix scene. They had learnt very soon the main rule of modern Grand Prix racing—that you follow the herd and conform, and do not experiment with natty engines or gearboxes. If you do, you get your hands burnt. It's a shame, but there it is.

From the first season, where their effort was far too fragile and, indeed, even rather slow, they progressed to the second where the cars were much more reliable and quicker to boot. If Revson had not been killed, who is to say that they would not have gained their first win *before* 1975.

It would be nice to see an American car win the Championship for there have been some valiant efforts at a class of racing which is not indigenous to that country. If it could not be Gurney winning with that beautiful engine, perhaps it could be Shadow with their sinister black cars.

Results

Year and race	DN1/1A	DN1/2A	DN1/3A	DN1/4A	DN1/5A	DN1/6A
1973						
South African GP	Oliver R	Follmer 6				
International Trophy	Oliver R	Follmer 6				
Spanish GP	Oliver R	Follmer 3	Hill R			
Belgian GP	Oliver C	Follmer R	Hill 9			
Monaco GP		Follmer P/C	Hill R	Oliver 10		
Swedish GP			Hill R	Oliver R	Follmer 14	
French GP			Hill 10	Oliver R	Follmer R	
British GP			Hill R	Oliver C	Follmer C	
Dutch GP			Hill 12	Oliver C	Follmer 10	Oliver S
German GP			Hill 13		Follmer C	Oliver 8
Austrian GP			Hill R	Oliver R		Follmer R
Italian GP			Hill 14	Oliver 11	Follmer 10	Oliver P
Canadian GP			Hill 16		Follmer 17	Oliver 3
United States GP			Hill 13	Redman D	Follmer 14	Oliver 15
1974						
Argentine GP						Jarier C
Brazil GP					Jarier R	

Results

Year and race	Chassis number and result				
	DN3/1A	DN3/2A	DN3/3A	DN3/4A	DN3/5A
1974					
Argentine GP	Revson C				
Brazil GP	Revson R				
Race of Champions	Revson 6	Jarier P/C			
International Trophy		Jarier 3			
Spanish GP		Jarier 15	Redman 7		
Belgian GP		Jarier 13	Redman 17/R		
Monaco GP		Jarier 3	Redman C	Jarier P	
Swedish GP		Jarier 5	Roos R	Jarier P	
Dutch GP		Jarier R	Pryce C	Jarier P	
French GP		Jarier 12	Pryce C	Jarier P	
British GP		Jarier R			Pryce 8
German GP		Jarier 8			Pryce 6
Austrian GP		Jarier 8		Jarier P	Pryce R
				Pryce P/C	
Italian GP		Jarier R	Pryce 10		Pryce P
Canadian GP		Jarier R			Pryce 19
United States GP		Jarier 10			Pryce 15
1975					
Argentine GP			Pryce 12		
Brazil GP			Pryce C		

C=Crash; D=disqualified; NQ=non-qualifier; P=practice car only; R=retired; S=spare car not used

Surtees

TS7, TS9 and TS14

Type	TS7
Year of construction	1970
Number made	2
Frame designer	Len Terry and John Surtees
Frame	Riveted aluminium monocoque with engine forming rear of chassis
Front suspension	Lower wishbone, upper rocker arm operating inboard coil spring/damper units
Rear suspension	Lower wishbone, upper transverse link, two forward running radius arms with outboard coil spring/damper units
Engine make	Cosworth
Engine designer	Keith Duckworth with Mike Costin
Engine type	DFV
Engine capacity	2993cc
Cylinders	8 in 90° Vee formation
Bore and stroke	85.7mm x 64.8mm
Valves per cylinder	2 inlet per cylinder in Vee, 2 exhaust per cylinder laterally
Carburation	Lucas port fuel injection
Ignition	Lucas OPUS system
Sparking plugs	1 centrally placed 10mm plug per cylinder
Camshafts per bank	2 overhead
Gearbox	Hewland DG300
Brakes	Front outboard discs, rear inboard discs

Surtees TS7/001   Surtees won the fourth race in a car of his own manufacture —the 1970 Oulton Park Gold Cup Race

Type	TS9
Years of construction	1971-2
Number made	6
Chassis details	as TS7
Engine details	as TS7
Gearbox	Hewland FG400
Brakes	as TS7
Type	TS14
Years of construction	1972-3
Number made	5
Frame designer	Len Terry and Len Terry
Frame	Compressed glass fibre, foam and aluminium layer monocoque with lateral deformable structure, engine forms rear part of frame
Front suspension	Double wishbone with outboard coil spring/damper units
Rear suspension	Lower wishbone, upper transverse link, two forward running radius arms with outboard coilspring/damper units
Engine details	as TS7
Gearbox	Hewland FG400
Brakes	External discs

Although basically a shy man, John Surtees likes things done his way. Crossing over from motor cycles to cars in the early 1960s he soon demonstrated an equivalent brilliance on four wheels. In 1964 he was the first and only man to win both a two-wheeler and four-wheeler World Championship when he won the World Driver's Championship in a Ferrari, but after that things went wrong. He left Ferrari in 1966, following a disagreement about how the Formula 1 team should be run. After a short spell in the big Cooper, which was too heavy in the engine department for even Surtees to do anything about, he had a similar experience with the Honda and the BRM. So he eventually decided—as Brabham, Gurney and McLaren had done before him—that if you want to do things your way the only answer is to run your own team. So in 1970 that is just what Surtees did. He could not finish his Formula 1 car until the middle of the year, although he had been constructing Formula 5000 cars since 1969, so for the first half of the season he made do with an old McLaren.

TS7 001   Revealed at the 1970 British GP, the Surtees followed fairly closely a number of British manufacturers who had started making Formula 1 cars now that the Cosworth engine and Hewland gearbox were freely available. It had a riveted aluminium monocoque chassis with the engine forming the rear of the chassis. The front suspension was by upper rocker arms (working inboard springs) and lower wishbones while the rear suspension was standard. Brakes were inboard at the rear. For a new effort the car did very well, after slight problems in practice, and worked its way up to seventh in the race before the engine bearings failed.

Surtees was troubled at the outset with engine problems, possibly because Cosworth were a bit stretched at the time with several new firms in action. The German GP at Hockenheim saw a further engine failure when Surtees had climbed right up to ninth place, while in Austria it was the camshaft gear teeth that stripped when he was lying seventh.

But at Oulton Park it all came right and, from being fastest in practice by three seconds when he was the only driver to get a completely dry flying practice lap, Surtees dominated the meeting.

Surtees TS9/001   The classic Surtees arrow shape was retained for the TS9 at first showing

He won the first heat and was second to Rindt in the second, obtaining overall victory in spite of incipient crown wheel and pinion failure.

Practice for the Italian GP saw one of Surtees' few structural failures when the rear suspension pulled away from its mounting. Luckily the second car of the series had been finished and the rear end of this was grafted on to the front end of 001. Leaking fuel before the start and an electrical problem meant that Surtees could only complete one lap.

The car gained its first points in Canada where, after an early stop when the engine was misfiring, Surtees carried on to a good fifth place. He drove well in the other two American races; he was sixth when the flywheel shattered at Watkins Glen and in Mexico had to settle for eighth place after the clutch packed up.

Surtees was quick to introduce a new model incorporating the lessons of the TS7; the first of the new series appeared at the 1971 South African GP. Thereafter the TS7s took a back seat as development was concentrated on the new cars. In 1971 Brian Redman had taken up temporary immigrant status in South Africa where he drove 001 for Surtees in the Grand Prix. He had an uneventful drive and nearly finished in the money.

Back in England use of the car was confined to drivers whose temporary position with the team was politically or economically desirable. In the International Trophy the seat was given to Alan Rollinson, the Formula 5000 star, who did not disgrace himself with a sixth place in the Formula 1 class. In the Dutch GP, Gijs van Lennep, the young Dutch driver later to find his niche in Formula 5000, was given a whirl and finished a very respectable eighth. Derek Bell, who seems to have been around for ever, was allocated 001 in the British GP but, after a promising show in practice, Surtees let him drive one of the newer TS9s in the race. 001's final Formula 1 appearance was in the paddock at the German GP where Dieter Quester was supposed to drive it, but the necessary finance was not forthcoming and the car never turned a wheel. This was probably no bad thing, for Quester's chief asset was bravery as was shown to good advantage in the Formula 2 slipstreaming battles which were all the rage at the time.

TS7 002 The companion for 001 revealed one or two slight modifications from the existing design when it appeared in

Austria for the Grand Prix. It was a little lower and lighter, with titanium hubs. Surtees used it first in practice for the Italian GP but it was cannibalised when 001 started falling to bits at the back.

Surtees had hoped to enter the three American races together with Derek Bell. He was somewhat chastened, to say the least, when the Canadian and Mexican entries for Bell were refused. On arrival in Canada he was then told that he should have brought 002 as well because he could have had a start for Bell. It was all a bit galling! So it was only in the United States GP that Bell got a drive and he did very well to get into the points with a good sixth place.

It was now into 1971 but for 002 not very long. Surtees had finished his TS9, but the second one was not ready until the Spanish GP so his No. 2 driver had to use the TS7 for a couple of races. Although it did not appear so at the time, it is now obvious that Surtees must have been running on a very tight budget and had really no say in who should be his second driver—it depended on which one could bring the largest bag of gold with him. In 1971 this turned out to be the German Rolf Stommelen, and a lot worse drivers than that might have turned up at the backdoor. Stommelen transferred across from the Brabham team where he had finished in tenth place in the 1970 World Driver's Championship. He brought a large amount of sponsorship from a German magazine, *Auto Motor und Sport*, and the caravan firm of Eifelland Wohnwagenbau. A singleton entry was made for Stommelen in the Argentine GP and he amazed one and all by leading the first heat from start to finish. It was a great shame when he collided with Amon in the second heat and broke some of the bolts holding the gearbox to the engine so that the rear suspension was unsupported.

Stommelen's second and final race in the TS7 was in the South African GP when the best he could do was a disappointing twelfth.

The first race appearance of the TS9 marked the final showing of the TS7. Maybe it had not set the world on fire, but it had done its job well. It had held together and even won one race. One could not wish for more in the first season of a new constructor.

TS9 001 When the new car appeared it did not differ radically from what had been seen before. It was a bit lower and a bit stronger, and was fitted with the Hewland FG400 gearbox which was much lighter than the Hewland DG300 the team had previously used. Surtees' usual luck with a new car persisted and, after running in a fine second place, the oil pipe to the gearbox cooler fractured and the gearbox seized solid.

Back to England and Brands Hatch for the annual pre-season gallop over the bumps of Kent where, despite the engine over-heating, the car went well and Surtees finished second. Up north at Oulton Park, the engine failed altogether. There was some confusion at the time when some thought that Surtees used 002 at Oulton Park; what probably happened was that he did, but in a private test session the week after driving 001 in the race itself.

Both cars, therefore, were now complete and Surtees kept the prototype for the Spanish GP where he finished an uncharacteristic eleventh after a stop to have the nose cone replaced. Surtees continued for the major part of the 1971 season with a mixture of retirements and middle of the field placings. A potential high placing in the International Trophy was spoiled when a pin in the front suspension broke, and in the Monaco GP, suffering from defective brakes, Surtees finished seventh.

The car was slightly modified for the Rhein-Pokalrennen; a relocated oil tank gave better cooling to the inboard rear brakes and new lighter wheels were fitted. A third place was the result, and finishes were recorded at the next four races—the highlights being a fifth place in the Dutch GP and a sixth in the British.

Following the German GP, Surtees took over one of the newer cars while Stommelen, having problems with his own car, used 001 in the Austrian GP where he finished seventh. The car's final appearance was in the Italian GP where in practice Stommelen had the alarming experience of a tyre coming off its rim followed by the inevitable crash. He was uninjured but the car was a write-off, the bits being used to relocate the radiator of the new 005 to the front.

TS9 002 Stommelen's new car was ready for the Spanish GP where he had the misfortune to get some dirt in the fuel system which caused his retirement from the race. This problem was sorted out in time for the Monaco GP and Stommelen took a good sixth place. In the Rhein-Pokalrennen, organised in memory of Jochen Rindt, Stommelen finished seventh after he had been penalised for being a naughty boy and missing the chicane. At

least this was better than the Dutch GP where he was disqualified for using outside assistance to restart following a spin. Middle of the field placings in France and Germany were punctuated by a fine fifth place in the British GP, despite his spectacles being dislodged at one point by a flying stone.

In the German GP Stommelen had a pit-stop to complain of an obscure handling defect, and as this had not been corrected before the Austrian GP he decided to use 001 instead. When 002 was not taken to Monza, he was left without a drive in the race after 001 crashed.

Stommelen's final drive for the team was in the Canadian GP when the car overheated following a spin which displaced a water pipe. Before the United States GP Surtees had a competition to see who would drive the car in the race. The contestants were Gijis van Lennep, who had driven the TS7 previously, and Sam Posey, the American Formula 5000 driver. Posey won by three seconds but in the race was forced to retire with engine failure.

Back in England the car made its final appearance in the grandiose-titled World Championship Victory Race. Surtees, in almost his last Formula 1 appearance, drove the car to an uneventful sixth place. However, if sixth was the best the boss himself could do, it was plain that the days were past when the straight TS9 was competitive and now it was all up to the TS9A.

TS9 003 Sold direct to Team Gunston for John Love to drive, 003 appeared in only one genuine Formula 1 race—the South African races now being run more to Formula Libre lines than when the Repco-Brabhams used to do their stuff. In fact, the car did not have a very long career as Love, celebrating twenty-five years of competition motoring, had a bad crash in the 1971 Rand Summer Trophy. The car was repaired but Love suffered another bad crash when he punctured in the 1972 South African GP. Soon after this, Love recognised the inevitability of anno domini and hung up his Formula 1 gloves, replacing them with Formula 2 ones when he purchased a Formula 2 Chevron. The TS9 was sold to the Domingo brothers whose main claim to fame is that, being half Indian, they have been allowed to race in some South African events, but not at Kyalami.

TS9 004 The fourth in the series, which was identical to the first three, presented itself for inspection at the French GP as a spare car. Although not quite ready, it could have been used if necessary. At the British GP, when the two regular cars were going well, Derek Bell was allowed to race 004 but a radius rod mounting pulled free and he had to retire.

The car was initially intended as a spare, but was soon pressed into service. Surtees drove it in the Austrian GP when he retired with valve trouble.

As defending winner, Surtees travelled up to Oulton Park for the Gold Cup Race. Third in the first heat and first in the second, Surtees was placed first in the overall classification and so took home the fine Gold Cup, originally the Daily Dispatch Gold Cup, for the third time.

At the 1971 Italian GP, where Surtees had introduced another model, the new signing Mike Hailwood was given 004 to drive. S. M. B. Hailwood, one of the all-time greats of motor-cycle racing, had previously tried Formula 1 racing in 1965 without any great success. Now he was trying again with the backing of two seasons of Formula 5000 and was quite a different proposition. He had learnt how to handle power and picked a good circuit to try the Surtees, because he had got Monza taped. He had a fine fourth place, only fractions of a second behind the winner, having led the race on several laps.

Hailwood missed the Canadian GP because he was racing the Formula 2 Surtees at Albi as he had a chance of winning the European Formula 2 Championship—a chance which he later took. So Surtees drove the car in Canada and finished eleventh after a spin. Hailwood flew across for the United States GP, but crashed the car after suffering a puncture.

The season closed with the end-of-season romp round Brands Hatch where Hailwood disgraced himself by colliding with Peterson who was trying to overtake him.

004 still had a whole season's racing in front of it. Before the 1972 Argentine GP it was converted to TS9A specifications which meant, in essence, that it was fitted with side-mounted radiators in order to achieve a streamlined front. The car was destined for a new member of the team—Andrea de Adamich. Not at all the popular image of an Italian, de Adamich was bespectacled and very quiet. He had been racing for a long while, starting off in the ex-Jo Siffert BT10 Brabham, converted to Formula 3 specifications, and progressing through a variety of single seaters before landing some good sponsorship from Ceramica Pagnossin which enabled him to hire the Surtees for a year.

De Adamich started with a couple of poor races, collecting a detached fuel line in the Argentine and brake trouble in South Africa, but settled down to business with a fourth place in Spain which startled the *cognoscenti*. When he followed this up with a seventh place in the difficult Monaco GP, it was plain that the lad had something. The Belgian GP was a bit of a fiasco, ending when the engine blew, but from a small entry in the GP de Republica Italiana, de Adamich came through to a strong second place.

It was inevitable that de Adamich's car should not get the same attention as those of the main team and he settled down to some steady middle of the field drives. These were interrupted by the occasional retirement which was sometimes a violent one, as when he formed a sudden attachment to Dave Walker in the British GP and to Howden Ganley in the United States GP.

His best race of the season was in the World Championship Victory Race when he claimed a third place, and not by default either. De Adamich had fixed up to drive a Brabham in 1973 so his final race, and 004's, was the 1973 South African GP when he finished eighth.

Sadly his Formula 1 career was not to last much longer as he was the only driver to be injured in the Scheckter crash at the British GP and, although only suffering a broken leg, he retired from racing.

TS9 005 It was well known that Surtees had been planning something new for the 1971 Italian GP, but when the car came along there was not really very much to get excited about. It merely followed the modern trend to side-mounted radiators; and even these were converted back to front mounting, after practice, from the remains of Stommelen's car. In the race Surtees only managed four laps before the engine blew up. The Surtees cars have always been good and solid, without providing the startling innovations of, say, the Lotus 72, which enabled it to be a race-winner for five years, or the general perfection of the McLaren M23, which lifted it just above the average. Perhaps the trouble is that Surtees has never had a really brilliant designer on his staff.

The car was converted again to side radiators for the United States GP and in this form it remained. Surtees had two stops in the race with poor fuel pressure and finished seventeenth.

For 1972 Surtees resolved to give up driving and made only one or two further appearances. For his No. 1 driver for the year, he could do no better than sign Mike Hailwood after his splendid drive in the 1971 Italian GP. Hailwood was allotted 005 for the season. Like 004 and 006, it was fitted with the new full-width nose and variable rate springs by the time the South African GP was run. Hailwood brought a new breath of life to the team and although he crashed, when a bolt pulled out of the rear suspension, he was lying second at the time. As the leader later retired, it is fair to speculate on what the result might have been.

The British non-Championship Formula 1 races always provided a good chance for the hangers-on to pick up a few morsels, and Hailwood confirmed his South African effort with a fine second place in the Race of Champions. In the International Trophy things looked even better when he took the lead from Fittipaldi, but sadly it only lasted for a few laps as the car developed a water leak and, of course, the engine overheated. A couple more retirements followed—the one at Monaco not really being his fault as he was rammed from behind by Howden Ganley. It seemed at this time as if Ganley had some sort of hang-up about Surtees drivers !

Hailwood started to earn his money again when he came fourth in Belgium and followed this up with a sixth in the French GP. After two retirements he was again back towards the top when he finished fourth in Austria. The climax of the year, though, was at his old stamping ground of Monza where a superb drive culminated in second place.

The Canadian GP clashed once more with the Albi Formula 2 race, in which Hailwood drove as he again had a say in the Formula 2 Championship, so that although 005 was present in Canada as a spare it was never used. Another high placing was aborted at Watkins Glen when Hailwood encountered the spinning Mike Beuttler and had to retire as a result of the ensuing damage. The final race of the season, at Brands Hatch, saw a topsy-turvy situation when Hailwood was the last of the Surtees drivers to finish, having had to stop for dry-weather tyres to be fitted, which dropped him to ninth place.

The factory drivers now had the TS14 cars in readiness for the 1973 season and 005 had only one further appearance when it was loaned to Luis Bueno, the local champion, to obtain a twelfth place in the Brazil GP.

TS9 006 The third driver Surtees hired was the Australian master of the excuse, Tim Schenken, who had dominated the smaller classes of racing in his Merlyn, but never really fulfilled the promise in the highest Formula. The car was ready for the 1972 season and Schenken was in the points from the start with a fifth in the Argentine GP.

The pre-season try-outs at Brands Hatch and Silverstone were a happy hunting ground for Surtees in 1972. Schenken backed up Hailwood with a fifth place in the Race of Champions, while the boss took 006 to a good third in the International Trophy race.

This was the first time that Surtees had tried to run three cars throughout the year; though probably necessary on financial grounds, it certainly proved to be a strain on the team. This showed in Schenken's string of retirements and lower placings which were due to the inability to carry out continual improvements on the cars, at any rate not sufficiently to keep up with the opposition. Schenken joined Hailwood in the bent car stakes at Monaco and 006 did not have an incident-free race until the United States GP, when Sam Posey finished twelfth.

By the end of 1972 Surtees had already decided to promote his Formula 2 driver, Carlos Pace, the Brazilian who is one of the most underestimated drivers around today. Like Oliver, he has not always been lucky in his choice of drives, but when he has the machinery he can pedal with the best of them. He showed this straight away when he finished second in his first Formula 1 drive for Surtees at the 1972 World Championship Victory Race. As in the case of Hailwood, Pace was destined for the TS14, and 006 had only one more race when it was loaned to Lord Hesketh for James Hunt to drive in the 1973 Race of Champions. The omens were there if anyone cared to see them when Hunt came in second.

When one compares Surtees with certain other constructors it is apparent that his cars were not getting the detailed development that the others were. This may have been for financial reasons, but it was more likely that the trouble lay in Surtees himself. He would be the first to admit that he takes everything on his own shoulders unlike, say, Colin Chapman who has got the delegation of responsibility down to a fine art. Luckily Surtees' shoulders are broad and he soldiered on into 1973 with the TS14, which differed radically from his first efforts.

TS14 001 First appearing at Monza in 1972, 001 was driven by Surtees himself in his last Formula 1 appearance. Compared with previous efforts the car was a big advance. Regulations were being changed for the next year so that cars would have to incorporate a 'deformable structure' to protect the fuel tanks. The Surtees had this on each side of the chassis in the cockpit area; in conjunction with the radiators which were side mounted, this brought the width of the car almost out to the centre line of the wheels. The main chassis was constructed of a sandwich of aluminium, foam and fibre glass, compressed into a single layer. The suspension was also modified—the front suspension, like the rear, now having outboard coil spring/damper units. It was an inauspicious debut as Surtees retired with brake trouble and another problem—the tyres—which was to affect the team for the whole of the next season. Surtees could do nothing about this as he had no control over it, being contracted to Firestone. There were terrible problems with wheel vibration, which was so bad on occasions that his drivers could hardly see. Hailwood in particular seemed to be psychologically affected because he did not show the same fire as in the previous season.

The car was to have one more attempt in 1972, at the United States GP when Schenken was forced out of the race with a broken wishbone. Schenken left the team at the end of the season, or, since he did not really have anywhere to go, perhaps it might be better to say that he was eased out. With de Adamich also departing, the team consisted of Mike Hailwood and Carlos Pace. Their first race, at the beginning of 1973, was in Argentina, but 001 did not reappear until the South African GP when Hailwood used it for practice. In the race, both the main cars were crashed, so Hailwood was forced to use 001 in the Race of Champions. This was probably Hailwood's best showing of the year because he was well in the lead when he suddenly swerved off the long straight into the bank. It was thought that either the rear suspension had failed or a tyre had blown. It was such an unexpected and alarming crash that Hailwood's confidence must have been affected, as was shown by his later performances.

Funnily enough, and to any spectators this must have seemed surprising, the car was not too badly damaged and was repaired in time for Surtees' Formula 2 protégé, Jochen Mass, to drive in the British GP. This was the occasion of the famous Schekter pile-up; all three Surtees cars were involved in the débâcle and none could start in the re-run. Naturally Surtees was a bit pig-sick about the whole thing. He made several remarks about not trying to win two-hour races on the second lap and, of course, he was quite right. One of the differences between the Grand Prix driver and the Formula Ford driver is that the former normally knows where not to make a fool of himself. If a Grand Prix driver has a really serious accident, it is almost always a solitary one.

Although 001 missed the Dutch GP, it was repaired for Mass to drive in his own country's Grand Prix when he finished seventh. Mass only had one more drive in the car, although it was taken to two races as a spare but not used. He managed to obtain an entry for the United States GP, but suffered engine trouble when lying a satisfactory seventh.

TS14 002 Intended as Hailwood's car, 002 had a short and chequered career. It started in three races, but only completed nineteen laps in all before it was destroyed. In Argentina a half shaft broke after ten laps; in Brazil it only lasted seven before the fuel metering unit failed, and it was on the third lap of the South African GP that Hailwood had his pile-up. The car was not particularly fast and was in the middle of the field when the South African Dave Charlton spun in front of him. Hailwood ran over Charlton's nose cone and also spun, ending up facing backwards. Some of the drivers got past safely when along came Reggazoni, who was apparently already having problems of his own, and cannoned into Hailwood's car. His BRM split down the side and both cars burst into flames. Hailwood was out of his car in a trice, after his fire extinguishers put the flames out. But Reggazoni was unconscious in his car which was still blazing. Hailwood immediately dashed into the flames, undid Reggazoni's straps and pulled him out. It was an act of extreme bravery and undoubtedly saved Reggazoni's life.

TS14 003 Carlos Pace's car was also ready for the Argentine GP. In spite of two spins, due to bad springing, he managed to finish in tenth place. The springs were replaced for the South African GP, but now the engine would not rev properly. Like

Surtees TS9/006 During its career the TS9 changed shape radically. This is the final look—driven by Surtees in the 1972 International Trophy

Hailwood, Pace also left the race suddenly when a tyre punctured, and it took three catch fences to stop him.

The car was soon repaired and Pace was able to take part in the International Trophy race. He had a good drive through the field after being held up at the start, but a wheel came loose and he had to retire. Another retirement followed when a drive shaft broke in Spain, but it was the Belgian GP that was the nightmare, although Pace managed to finish the race. The handling of the car was not good to start with, but even so Pace was running in fourth place when one of the tyres started to creep round the rim. This upset the balance of the car and his wing collapsed. It was all a bit awkward, but he made it in eighth place.

The car was not used at Monaco and, between the Belgian and Swedish GPs, the handling problem was sorted out to a large extent. It was found that the anti-roll bar was causing interference with the front suspension movement. When this was corrected, things were a lot better and, in spite of the, by now, compulsory pit-stop for all Surtees cars to have new tyres fitted, Pace finished the next two races.

003's final race was the British GP; there it was the only one of the three Surtees to be completely written off in the accident. It was lucky that the crash happened when it did because at least Surtees had a spare car available which Pace was able to use.

TS14 004 The replacement for 002 was ready for Hailwood at the 1973 International Trophy, but there were tyre problems at Silverstone, a broken oil pipe in Spain and a crash in the Belgian GP, before a finish was obtained in Monaco. Hailwood had been in sixth place, but what with a puncture, no brakes, only half a gear lever and two collisions with guard rails, it is not surprising he dropped to eighth.

Two retirements followed—one due to further tyre trouble; then came the shunt at Silverstone. Hailwood's car was the least damaged and was ready again for the next race. For the British GP, Surtees modified the nose cones in an attempt to cure the chronic understeering that was a characteristic of the cars.

The rest of the season was in a similar vein: a small fire in Holland, four finishes in succession—just—and the inevitable tyre changes in almost every race. In the last race of the TS14s—the United States GP—the rear suspension collapsed. It was the final straw. Hailwood moved across to McLaren in 1974.

TS14 005 In between all the worries of a fraught season, Surtees managed to build up a spare car. Pace used it in the Monaco GP, but suffered a drive-shaft failure. After this it became the general spare and practice hack, until it was pressed into service following the big pile-up. It seemed to like the experience because it was the most successful of all the TS14s. In its first race as Pace's regular car the vibration was bad, and it got worse when a balance wheel fell off. Nevertheless a seventh place was obtained.

In Germany things were better and Pace really showed his potential class to all who cared to see, when he came up through the field to finish a great fourth. Not only this but he had a new lap record to show for his pains. Considering the race was round the difficult Nurburgring, he definitely gets an 'alpha' for effort. Even better was to come when he got third spot in Austria. The fuel pressure went to pot at the end, but he just staggered over the line in front of the fourth man.

At last it looked as if Surtees was getting somewhere in Formula 1 to compare with the success in Formula 2. But no, as so often in motor racing, the cup is raised to the lips only to be dashed away at the end. In Italy, from being in fifth spot, Pace had two punctures. It was the same story in Canada, while at the final race of the season he joined Hailwood in suffering rear suspension failure.

Pace stayed with the team for half of 1974 but gradually became disenchanted, finally leaving to join his friend Reutemann in the Brabham team.

When one looks at the first four years of what is really a typical constructor, one wonders how any team can ever win a race, let alone a Championship. The problems that Surtees had to overcome were tremendous. Like most other teams, he had severe problems with finance, but has been very lucky to form a long relationship with Lesney Matchbox Models. He has had problems with drivers—who has not—and he has even had problems with himself! He does take too much on himself. What is probably essential, if he is to get to the top, is for Surtees to recognise his own limitations and stick to them. If he had a really competitive car built for him to sort out and get race fit, he could beat anybody.

Surtees has been trying for six years and is close to success. There is no team I would like to see bring it off more than his.

Results

Year and race	Chassis number and result		
1970	TS7/001	TS7/002	
British GP	Surtees R		
German GP	Surtees 9		
Austrian GP	Surtees R		
Gold Cup Race	Surtees 1		
Italian GP	Surtees R	Surtees P	
Canadian GP	Surtees 5		
United States GP	Surtees R	Bell 6	
Mexican GP	Surtees 8		
1971			
Argentine GP		Stommelen C	
South African GP	Redman 7	Stommelen 12	
	Surtees P		
International Trophy	Rollinson 6		
Dutch GP	van Lennep 8		
British GP	Bell P		
German GP	Quester NS		

Results

Year and race	Chassis number and race					
1971	TS9/001	TS9/002	TS9/003	TS9/004	TS9/005	TS9/006
South African GP	Surtees R					
Race of Champions	Surtees 3					
Rothman's Trophy	Surtees R					
Spanish GP	Surtees 11	Stommelen R				
International Trophy	Surtees 8					
Monaco GP	Surtees 7	Stommelen 6				
Rhein-Pokalrennen	Surtees 3	Stommelen 7				
Dutch GP	Surtees 5	Stommelen D				
French GP	Surtees 8	Stommelen 11		Surtees P		
British GP	Surtees 6	Stommelen 5		Bell R		
				Surtees P		
German GP	Surtees 7	Stommelen 10		Stommelen P		
Austrian GP	Stommelen 7			Surtees R		
Gold Cup Race				Surtees 1		
Italian GP	Stommelen P/C			Hailwood 4	Surtees R	
Canadian GP		Stommelen R		Surtees 11		
United States GP		Posey R		Hailwood 15/C	Surtees 17	
		van Lennep NS				
World Championship VR		Surtees 6		Hailwood C		
1972						
Argentine GP				de Adamich R		Schenken 5

Results

Year and race	Chassis number and result					
1972	TS9/001	TS9/002	TS9/003	TS9/004	TS9/005	TS9/006
South African GP			Love P/C	de Adamich 19	Hailwood R	Schenken R
			Ferguson P			
Race of Champions					Hailwood 2	Schenken 5
International Trophy					Hailwood R	Surtees 3
Spanish GP				de Adamich 4	Hailwood R	Schenken 8
Monaco GP				de Adamich 7	Hailwood C	Schenken C
Gold Cup Race						Schenken 3
Belgian GP				de Adamich R	Hailwood 4	Schenken R
GP Repub. Ital.				de Adamich 2		
French GP				de Adamich 14	Hailwood 6	Schenken 17
British GP				de Adamich C	Hailwood R	Schenken R
German GP				de Adamich 12	Hailwood R	Schenken 13
Austrian GP				de Adamich 14	Hailwood 4	Schenken 11
Italian GP				de Adamich R	Hailwood 2	Schenken C
Canadian GP				de Adamich R	S	Schenken 7
United States GP				de Adamich C	Hailwood C	Posey 12
World Championship VR				de Adamich 3	Hailwood 9	Pace 2
1973						
Brazil GP					Bueno 12	
South African GP				de Adamich 8		
Race of Champions						Hunt 2

Results

Year and race	TS14/001	TS14/002	TS14/003	TS14/004	TS14/005
1972					
Italian GP	Surtees R				
United States GP	Schenken R				
1973					
Argentine GP		Hailwood R	Pace R		
Brazil GP		Hailwood R	Pace R		
South African GP	Hailwood P	Hailwood C	Pace C		
Race of Champions	Hailwood C				
International Trophy			Pace R	Hailwood R	
Spanish GP			Pace R	Hailwood R	
Belgian GP			Pace 8	Hailwood C	
Monaco GP			Pace P	Hailwood 8	Pace R
Swedish GP			Pace 10	Hailwood R	Pace P
French GP			Pace 13	Hailwood R	Pace P
British GP	Mass C		Pace C	Hailwood C	S
Dutch GP				Hailwood R	Pace 7
German GP	Mass 7			Hailwood 14	Pace 4
Austrian GP	S			Hailwood 10	Pace 3
Italian GP	S			Hailwood 7	Pace R
Canadian GP				Hailwood 9	Pace18/R
United States GP	Mass R			Hailwood R	Pace R

C=Crash ; D=disqualified ; NQ=non-qualifier ; P=practice car only ; R=retired ; S=spare car not used

Acknowledgements

It would not have been possible for me to write this book without the kind help of many people, all of whom I wish to thank most gratefully.

The other two members of the Formula One Register, John Thompson and Duncan Rabagliati, who have previously been mentioned, are almost co-authors. We have corresponded and talked for fifteen years about motor racing and, by comparing and exchanging information, have accumulated what we fondly believe to be a unique record of Grand Prix racing from 1954 to the present day.

For the vast majority of the illustrations I must thank the staff of *Autosport*. To the enthusiast, the magazine's files are like the crock of gold and permission to use its photographs is gratefully acknowledged. The exceptions are Plate 8, provided by Publifoto of Milan, and Plates 20 and 21 which were given to me by the manufacturers of the Shadow–Nicholls Advanced Vehicle Systems.

It would be impossible to keep records of the sort kept by the Formula One Register without the assistance of the various magazines devoted to motor racing. *Motor Sport* with its European correspondent, Denis Jenkinson, seldom makes errors of fact and is always the last word on doubtful points. *Motoring News* devotes more space in its reports to the 'also-rans', while *Autosport's* tabulated results, though not always 100-per-cent correct, are a marvel considering they arrive through the letter box just four days after an event. As far as the reporting of Grand Prix racing is concerned, these three magazines stand alone.

Last, but certainly not least, I must thank also my wife, Betty, whose patience is unlimited. First, she puts up with me writing and rewriting my records, and with being snapped at whenever she interrupts me. But, as she says, at least it keeps me out of the pubs. Secondly, she has suffered complete isolation while I have been behind closed doors typing the manuscript. Thirdly, after all this, she has read through the book and corrected my appalling English. If every other author is as fortunate as I am in his choice of spouse, he is a lucky man indeed.

Index of Personalities

Index of Cars